STAND UP, SPEAK OUT AGAINST WORKPLACE BULLYING

Your Guide to Survival and Victory Through 23 Real Life Testimonies

Compiled by
Catherine Mattice Zundel, MA, SPHR, SHRM-SCP,
Ms. Camay McClure and Sue Pai Yang, retired N.J.
Judge of Compensation of
The National Workplace Bullying Coalition

ISBN 978-1-4958-2117-2
ISBN 978-1-4958-2118-9 eBook

Published April 2018

INFINITY PUBLISHING
1094 New DeHaven Street, Suite 100
West Conshohocken, PA 19428-2713
Toll-free (877) BUY BOOK
Local Phone (610) 941-9999
Fax (610) 941-9959
Info@buybooksontheweb.com
www.buybooksontheweb.com

The National Workplace Bullying Coalition is a 501(c)3 nonprofit. Through education and mobilization we envision a future where workers are assured their right to dignity at work, where workplace bullying is an unlawful act and where employers have taken effective steps to prevent, detect and remedy acts of workplace bullying.

www.WorkplaceBullyingCoalition.org

Special Thanks to

Everyone who submitted their story. It took courage to share your personal journey of resilience, and the world needs to hear it.

Karla Cordova, Rebecca Del Secco, and all others who participated in helping the Coalition bring these important stories to light.

TABLE OF CONTENTS

INTRODUCTION

In my former life, I lived in a little one bedroom apartment three blocks from the beach. Fresh out of grad school, where I had been studying workplace bullying through an academic lens, with my nose buried in research articles from around the world, I was now free to research workplace bullying on the mainstream Internet.

I joined several chatrooms and groups for people who had been bullied just to see what was going on in them, and I didn't like what I saw. Not at all. Rather than proping each other up, these group members were bringing each other down. As one person would share their story of being bullied, others would jump in and inform this target that their life was over, they were doomed, and it was only a matter of time before their world came crashing down around them.

Having been through workplace bullying myself, I would often jump in and offer a more positive spin. I would share my own story of success, and I would write that if they could find ways to build their resilience – their ability to overcome adversity – that they could make it through. These comments were often met with anger, and I even felt a little bullied.

Naturally, I left these groups. They were a place people went to commiserate, and I'm not a commiserater. I am always focused on action because I believe if you change your actions, you can change the game.

It was then, all those years ago, that I conceived the idea for this book. I realized that we needed to change the conversation about workplace bullying online. We need to help targets understand that there is hope, and there is a way out. It was only now that I could achieve this vision through the National Workplace Bullying Coalition.

And if you read that previous paragraph thinking to yourself that I must deliusional, consider this famous quote: *When we are no longer able to change a situation, we are challenged to change ourselves.*

That quote comes from Viktor Frankl, who was trapped in concentration camps during the Holocaust. Through his very unique perspective as a neurologist and psychiatrist, he noticed that people in these camps were all handling it very differently: some gave up, others unequivocally believed they would survive. When I'm in bad situations, I think of this quote and these survivors – if they could believe in all that death around them that they would get through it, I can believe it too.

Resilience is a mindset. Believe. Believe you can get through workplace bullying. Believe there are many others before you who have done just that.

In fact, 23 of us have gathered here in this book to help you. Read our stories, learn from us. And if you find yourself in a group where people are telling you it's hopeless, leave the group. Stick with people who are feeding you the right narratives – the ones where you come out on top.

Catherine Mattice Zundel, MA, SPHR, SHRM-SCP

ONE

MASTER OF MY OWN DESTINY
Catherine Mattice Zundel

I was the Director of Human Resources for a non-profit organization. "The bully" was my peer, also director level and we both reported directly to the president. I noticed immediately after I started working there that Tom (whose name has been changed) was insubordinate to the president. During staff meetings for example, Tom would interrupt him and say disdainfully, "No, that's not what we're doing, geez," or, "You're giving the wrong information," as if the president didn't know what he was talking about. These little bouts of insubordination were just the beginning of a five-year hell.

Tom targeted almost everyone in the office, including me. He was an uber-excessive micromanager, even to people he didn't manage and who were not in his department. He yelled frequently, and had a way of staring people down to make them crumble. He talked down to everyone.

He even made life difficult for clients and for the people who referred us business. In fact, clients and referral sources secretly came to me for help in order to avoid him. It wasn't my job to help them, but I didn't want to lose customers or referrals so I helped them anyway. Of course, this got me into deeper hot water with "the bully" because when he discovered I'd done part of his job behind his back, he was of course angry and the bullying got worse.

Part of Tom's job was to order and manage the distribution of office supplies, so even something as simple as getting a pad of Post-its® was a traumatic experience. Whenever I realized I needed a new pad of paper for example, it took me all morning to mentally prepare to go down to his office and ask for it. My (and everyone's) requests were always met with a huffy, "What happened to the pad of paper I gave you a few weeks ago?" To which I'd reply, "I used it to do my work." To which he'd reply, "Well what were you doing? What work required the pad?" Of course, all of this interrogation was a massive waste of time. I know this isn't that bad when I think of other workplace bullying stories I've heard, but to be honest, I've blocked most of my experiences from my memory.

Not only did I personally deal with the repercussions of this behavior, but as the Director of HR, I dealt with the organizational repercussions too. I frequently took employee grievances to the president in order to get his assistance in ending the bullying, but his response was always, "That's just how he is, people shouldn't let him get to them." Bullying was legal and wasn't against our corporate policy so my hands were tied; I couldn't help.

Looking back, I think the President was afraid of "the bully" too. I can still hear him saying, "Why can't you just be the bigger person?" as if he was pleading with me to let it go so he wouldn't have to stand up to "the bully" himself.

About three years into the job I started graduate school at San Diego State University studying organizational communication. Early on in the program I had a class called the "Dark Side of Communication," where we learned about negative human interactions (e.g., stalking, domestic violence, sibling rivalry, etc.). Of course, we had to write a paper on something dark, so I chose to write about my situation at work. It was during this time in 2004 that I came across the phrase "workplace bullying" and saw that there were 25 years of academic research on the topic from around the world. As I read more and more articles, I was mesmerized. Everything I was reading lined up with my situation. I now had confirmation that I wasn't crazy and I knew then that Tom was indeed a bully. My situation was real.

After that, every ounce of research I did in graduate school was on workplace bullying. I even did my thesis paper on workplace bullying and dedicated it to "The Post-it® Nazi." (He knows I dedicated it to him, by the way.) I joke that I have a Master's degree in workplace bullying.

Dealing with bullying directed at me and the turnover and poor morale the bullying caused others eventually took its toll on me. My performance suffered and I was on the brink of depression. I actually had a sign over my alarm clock that said, "Get up!" on it, as if I needed a reminder to get out of bed.

My performance suffered tremendously. After five years the president and I decided it would be best if we parted ways. Actually, he came to me one day and asked why my performance had deteriorated so much. I burst into tears and found myself giving a 30-day notice because I knew I couldn't take the abuse any longer. His response: "If you're that unhappy, you should leave now." So, he watched as I packed my things and left with my tail between my legs.

I vividly remember the drive home from work that day. I didn't expect to be jobless at that point in my life. I was still finishing out graduate school and hadn't prepared for this. Despite that, I honestly and truly and wholeheartedly felt relief. Literally, not figuratively, the colors in the sky were brighter. I could feel my shoulders roll back up as the weight on them was lifted. I didn't know what would happen to me, but I felt a thousand percent better.

Luckily I had a friend who owned a condo with plenty of room and she let me live there rent free until I landed on my feet. After six months or so I obtained a job doing HR and project management at a start-up tech firm. I worked there for about nine months, but the investor pulled the next round of funding and several of us were laid off.

Again, I found myself driving home with no idea how I would pay my rent. I distinctly remember walking in the door, opening up my laptop, purchasing a website domain called "noworkplacebullies.com," and pouring my heart into the website. Everything I knew about workplace bullying at the time went on that webpage. A few months later, the International Association for Workplace Bullying and Harassment (www.IAWBH.org) was having a conference, so I submitted my thesis paper and bought my ticket. And there I was, telling people I was building a consulting business around workplace bullying.

Now, all these years later, I am indeed an HR consultant who specializes in workplace bullying. I have been cited as an expert on workplace bullying in USA Today, Huffington Post, Washington Times, Entrepreneur Magazine, and Psychology Today. I have appeared on NPR, FOX, ABC, NBC, and Al Jazeera. I've written articles that have been published in over 45 trade magazines, and even one in Japan. I've spoken at about 100 conferences on the topic of resolving workplace bullying, likely touching about 20,000 HR professionals. I've served a huge array of clients from the third largest energy company in the world down to small businesses and nonprofits.

The point is that I'm okay. I'm more than okay. I made it through and I'm a stronger and better person because of my experience. I can thank my bully for the gift he's given me – something to be passionate about. I am my own boss, I love what I do, and I enjoy helping others solve a problem I couldn't solve when I was a Director of HR.

Speaking of HR, I want to provide some insight into their world. They get a bad reputation for not helping targets of bullying and maliciously being on the employer's side. While that may be true for some, please know there are many out there who want to help. Just to give you an example of their experience dealing with workplace bullying, in two separate cases I've received a call from an HR professional who was seeking help because there had been a workplace suicide, and the notes were both about workplace bullying. In both cases, I put together a proposal for services to change the culture and in both cases, the leaders said solving bullying wasn't a priority for them and my services were rejected. I've also received calls from many other HR professionals desperately seeking advice about how to convince the leaders they needed to solve the bullying. There are many HR professionals out there who DO CARE.

Help HR help you by giving them solid, tangible facts that they can tie to a corporate policy. Help them provide clear and tangible information to leaders about the damage the bullying is causing. Provide quantifiable information such as the cost of turnover in your department, or the cost of a lost customer. Help HR make their case to leaders that the bullying needs to stop. If the leaders don't want to solve the problem, then leave. Your sanity and dignity is worth so much more than the paycheck. Have faith that you will land on your feet.

Learn everything you can about workplace bullying. Doing that saved me. Helping others has saved me.

And stay strong. You can, and you will, survive.

FIVE PIECES OF ADVICE:

1. Don't give up. There IS a light at the end of the tunnel. It may be hard to see now, but it's there.
2. Hold your head up high. Your body language at work is showing your feelings of defeat and feeding into them. Walk with your head held high, your shoulders back, and your toes pointed forward. Your body and mind are connected – use your body to show confidence and your brain will get the message.
3. Read everything you can get your hands on about personal resilience, confidence,

self-esteem, and adversity. Arm yourself with the knowledge you need to live a life of resilience.

4. Let the bully fuel your passion for life. Take all the anger, hurt, frustration, loneliness, and confusion and turn those emotions into a new and better you.

5. If you've stood up for yourself against the bully, and filed a complaint with HR, and nothing's resolved, then leave. You have to take care of you.

Catherine Mattice Zundel is founder of Civility Partners (www.CivilityPartners.com), an HR consulting firm focused on solving the problem of workplace bullying by replacing it with a positive workplace culture. Her clients include the third largest energy company in the world; the U.S. Marine Corps and U.S. Navy; several hospitals and universities; and many government agencies, nonprofits, and businesses in a huge array of industries. She has made many news appearances, authored numerous articles, and has spoken on the topic around the world. She has authored two books, "BACK OFF! Your Kick-Ass Guide to Ending Bullying at Work," which Ken Blanchard called "the most comprehensive and valuable handbook on the topic," and, "SEEKING CIVILITY: How Leaders, Managers and HR Can Create a Workplace Free of Bullying." She was fortunate enough to connect with the National Workplace Bullying Coalition as it was being conceived, and is currently serving as its President.

You can connect with Catherine at:
- *Catherine@CivilityPartners.com*
- *http://civilitypartners.com*
- *https://www.linkedin.com/in/catherinemattice*
- *https://twitter.com/catmattice*
- *https://www.facebook.com/CivilityPartners*

TWO

BEAUTY FOR ASHES
Ms. Camay McClure, NSA

My legal career began in 2003 when I decided to enroll in college and get a degree because I wanted to invest in my career, not just get another job. I held various support positions with several firms before my prayers were answered in 2011, when I received a phone call from a recruiter for an insurance company's Staff Counsel Office.

My credentials qualified me for a litigation paralegal position and after a two-and-a-half-hour interview, federal background check, drug test, credit check, and reference check, I was offered the position. I felt like I hit the lottery! I was so excited to make a contribution to the office, essentially supporting those in litigation. This was something I was able to relate to personally. I was even more excited to learn about my professional role as a paralegal and take my career to the next level.

I supported two attorneys consistently, often stepping up when asked by Lead Counsel to support an additional attorney during bouts of staff turnover. I was supporting Lead Counsel and being mentored by her, engaging myself in other platforms within the corporation. I was the office lead for a project the company sponsored, raising awareness about domestic violence around the country. I was also the office lead for engaging staff in making annual charitable donations for their Giving Back Campaign. I participated in interoffice decisions regarding innovative processes and program suggestions for the paralegal team in Seattle. This was often incorporated into paralegal processes throughout our corporate region. My career was launching into a phase I was super excited about! I never imagined the environment would take a ninety-degree turn down a fatal path.

Lead Counsel, the attorney who hired me, was promoted to Regional Counsel in the Midwest. Corporate Leadership decided to promote one of the staff attorneys into the Lead Counsel position and in a matter of months, I found myself confused and bewildered at her blatant aggression towards me. I never supported her during my employment, and we never really interacted with each other. But she slowly began to question my abilities as a litigation paralegal, scrutinizing my every move. In the beginning, I thought she was experiencing trust issues, as now she was Lead Counsel and expected to manage the office.

On several occasions, she told me that the work product I was generating and processing religiously were suddenly being done wrong. I remember when she gave me my first 6-month review that was rated "not meeting expectations." I asked for case specific details that I could research and was given the opportunity to dispute my review rating. I provided documentation to rebuke her theory to the HR Department, only for her to tell me she refused to remove the inaccuracies and would not reevaluate my rating. She didn't apologize for being incorrect, nor did she ever stop micro-managing my every move. In fact, she became more aggressive in her behaviors and began secluding me from the paralegal team.

I vividly remember one of the first conversations I had with her, regarding her trust issues and controlling tendencies. She tried to tell me in a meeting that all of the attorneys in the office didn't trust me, which I quickly confronted her about. I believe this conversation is when she made up her mind to target me. I wasn't going to accept her inappropriate exaggerated opinion. I forced her to admit she was speaking in a general sense, when in fact, she was the only one who had a trust issue with me. The other attorneys she tried to refer to had never worked with me, and in fact, were all brand new attorneys in our office. I honestly thought this conversation was going to be the bridge that brought us together, giving us both a better understanding and mutual respect for each other. Boy, was I wrong!

The next conversation was related to a specific case and a long-standing process in our office.

When she asked me what process I followed, I referenced our office policy, which I followed. She yelled at me, telling me she was so mad at me she could barely talk to me. She also advised me this incident was going to be in my review, which was scheduled for the following week. Then she ended the meeting. I was blown away. I couldn't believe how she yelled at me and threatened my job. I knew when I walked into the office Monday morning, I had to report the incident.

The next 6 months were the worst progression of grief I have ever experienced, with the exception of losing my mother in 2008. I guess the difference is I only experienced my mother dying once. I was experiencing being bulled every single day, sometimes several times a day. This woman was documenting inaccurate accounts of my work product and work ethic. Every time I was able to provide written documentation to discredit her and reveal her inaccuracies to the HR department, she grew bolder, rallied other staff members and completely isolated me from the team. The first six-month review she issued to me reflected less than acceptable work performance. It indicated several work product or project management errors, which were completely inaccurate. I provided documented proof to the HR department again, proving her bullying behaviors and now, retaliatory reactions for reporting her. Even though the HR department agreed with the inaccuracies, she was never forced to remove them from my review and re-evaluate my performance. In fact, she looked me straight in my face and told me she refused to remove the inaccurate information and re-evaluate me.

I remember that time in my life very vividly. I doubt I will ever forget the torture and abuse I suffered and how it rattled my spirit and my sense of peace. I was being terrorized every day by a woman who unapologetically bullied me. She creatively manipulated others in the office who went along with her tactics to ensure they never became a target. I would get up in the morning, commute an-hour-and-a-half to Seattle, work for eight hours in a war zone, then commute an-hour-and-a-half back home. I would go straight to bed and get up the next morning to do it all over again. I was mentally exhausted. I suffered from panic attacks every other day. I became reclusive and ceased all outside human interaction. My face appeared weak and atrophied. I was suffering. My suffering affected my family and close friends. It was very hard for them to watch the progression of grief take over my life. I was on a dangerous downhill spiral and needed help. I was ready to take my own life.

I have asked myself many times over the years how I survived the bullying and retaliation. I wasn't able to identify the situation with a certain diagnosis or label. It wasn't until I became connected with a thought provoking master and alchemist who told me I was being bullied. She began to describe my manager like she had worked with her. What she was doing was describing this woman's behavior and my feelings and emotions as responses to those behaviors. I felt like she was right there, a fly on the wall, watching it all. It was in that moment that I saw a glimpse of faith. I now was able to identify what I was going through, which gave me the power to address it. I knew I needed to see a medical doctor and begin building my support system to fight this battle. The day came when my doctor immediately pulled me out of work. I was having visions of throwing her off the twenty-second floor of the building. I pictured throwing her through the corner window in her cubicle and walking to the edge to witness her demise. This was a dangerous situation. I am thankful each and every day that someone saved me.

There are countless other incidents that took place over a period of nine months that cannot possibly be narrated in this chapter but do include, being out on short-term disability for four months, returning to the office and being terminated four months later for "misconduct." I was evicted from my home, lost everything I owned and a year later lost my unemployment appeal. She raped me of my long standing successful employment position, stripped me of my relationship with my peers, and prevented me from moving on in the company ever again.

Today, I have completely recovered from all of my losses. I am still recovering financially from the whole ordeal, but that too will be restored. I have been equipped with valuable tools and resources to utilize in my business that help others end bullying in the workplace. That is a blessing that cannot be measured. I have exposed one of the most dangerous epidemics in our country to millions of people across several social media platforms and I have used my voice to speak out. I have taken back my power and have learned thought provoking skills that build my sense of power and my ability to maintain it. I want to share six vital steps with you in an effort to help you, the reader, begin to claim victory over your personal situation of being bullied.

SIX PIECES OF ADVICE:

1. Document Factual Incidents. Document what happened, who said what and who was present. When pulled into a meeting or private conversation, take a note pad with you and take notes. Write down what is being said to you in the meeting.
2. Leave Your Feelings Out of It. If you are asked a question in the meeting, respond with, "I will have to check on that and get back to you." Use an open-ended response to allow yourself the opportunity to follow up with them. I will explain more on this below.

3. *Always Follow Up in Writing.* Once you have had an opportunity to research and well document your response to questions you've been asked, you will respond in an email. The email should reiterate the meeting details, which should be easy because you took notes the entire meeting and didn't say anything yourself. You will provide your promised responses, attaching any documentation or evidence needed to support or highlight your response.

4. Stay Engaged with Your Agenda. If you had questions or requested clarification on something, follow up in writing. Go back to the original email you sent, forward it on, and save all drafts. What you're doing here is creating a documented paper trial and you're keeping all conversations in writing. This will help you in the future when you need to establish the false allegations about you.

5. *Seek Medical Attention and Build Your Support System.* Medical professionals and experts are the only people who can diagnose you with any medical condition or mental health disability. Your primary care doctor will evaluate you, make a determination about your needed medical health and work with other doctors and experts to develop an appropriate treatment plan for you.

6. Hold Human Resources Accountable. When you are diagnosed with a mental health issue, you now become an American who is protected under the ADA Act as a person with a disability. This legally forces your employer to consider any special medical related requests on your behalf. The law does not require your employer to grant any request; however, the secret here is to make reasonable requests that you know your employer can agree to or has granted to others.

Being bullied in the workplace is nothing to take lightly. It should never be discounted or dismissed and should always be reported. When other employees witness bullying in the workplace, they are emotionally effected too, which violates human rights and their entitlement to a safe and civil workplace, absent of bullying and retaliation. It is our responsibility to speak up, defend targets from being bullied in the workplace and report all bullying behaviors.

Ms. Camay McClure is the CEO of Ms. Camay International, LLC, a professional legal consulting and notary signing company supporting Ms. Camay's passion and commitment to inspire people across the nation and around the world. She is a Kaplan University graduate, completing her undergraduate degree in Paralegal Studies, headed to Law School. Ms.

Camay spent two successful seasons live on the air as a Radio Personality on The Ms. Camay Show on Seattle's own KKNW 1150AM. She is a National Lifetime Title Holder in Plus Size Pageantry, Plus Size Model and Senior Paralegal Professional, harnessing 14 years of commercial litigation experience under her crown.

An International Best Selling Author in the Anthology, "Family Ties : What Binds Us & Tears Us Apart", her journey is one that has required great courage, recently directing a black tie fashion gala in Seattle, Washington that broke the silence around workplace bullying. Ms. Camay is a Humanitarian Award Recipient being honored for her efforts as an advocate in her community and for the American workforce, passionate about eliminating bullying from the workplace through education, awareness and legislation.

You can connect with Ms. Camay at:
- www.mscamay.com
- www.mscamayinternational.com
- www.themscamayshow.com
- www.facebook.com/mscamay.com
- www.facebook.com/mscamayinternational
- www.facebook.com/themscamayshow
- @LifetimeQueen
- @MsCIntllc
- @TheMsCamayShow

THREE

Epiphanies
Marisa Wood

Standing at the bus stop on a cold November night, I could still hear the song "Ventura Highway" in my mind. It had come on Pandora that night at just the right moment: when my resolve to walk away from a toxic job was failing me. It reminded me there was a whole world out there, beyond the windowless walls of a cramped office, beyond my boss's verbal abuse and beyond sixty-hour work weeks. It reminded me of freedom—and at last, after sixteen months in hell, I was free. I'd left my office keys and a brief resignation letter on my desk, in an envelope with my boss's name on it.

In the sixteen months that I'd been the HR person for that childcare center, I'd sacrificed time for friends and hobbies to meet unreasonable expectations. I was not a manager, and yet I was expected to be available to my boss 24 hours a day, 7 days a week, with no overtime pay. Two months before I quit, I'd gone on a Saturday hiking trip to the North Cascades with friends — only to find four voice mail messages from my boss telling me to call her as soon as I got them. When I called her the next morning, I discovered she wasn't calling about something urgent — it was something trivial that could have waited until Monday.

I'd put in sixty hours a week and taken work home with me, both to meet impossible deadlines and to prevent my boss's constant nitpicking and unpredictable outbursts of anger. She often failed to communicate her expectations to me — then would shift the blame to me and berate me when I failed to meet them. She triangulated me with other employees, saying other people had complained about me but never specifically naming names. And, when I didn't do something she wanted, she would either accuse me of not caring about my job — or worse, threaten to replace me. She also threatened that if she fired me, I wouldn't get unemployment, because she always contested unemployment claims and she always won.

Despite her threats about not getting unemployment, and despite the poor job market, I'd almost walked off the job four or five times before. Each time my boss lured me back in with promises I now know she never intended to keep: of a more reasonable work schedule, of writing projects she was going to have me work on, of outsourcing payroll to lower my stress level. That stress level had gotten to the point where we'd had several discussions about its effects on my health, and a doctor had advised me, just a month before I quit, that my current situation was "unsustainable and bad for [my] health." I was having panic attacks three or four times a week, and crying before, after, and eventually during work. Finally - after one particularly horrible incident of verbal abuse, in which I was blamed for a handyman's failure to complete a job I hadn't even known my boss had asked him to do until he walked in the door - the doctor advised me it was time to leave. He agreed to write me a letter to give to the unemployment office.

Now, safely back at my apartment after walking away from all that, I began catching up on all the sleep I'd missed. I was physically and mentally exhausted from my time in hell, and I spent most of the next two or three weeks following my doctor's orders to rest.

The Thanksgiving holiday came, and with it, some much-needed time with family. My stepmother and my Aunt Jan encouraged me to apply for unemployment benefits, since I'd quit on the advice of a doctor, and in our state, quitting for health reasons was considered "good cause." When I came back from my Thanksgiving visit, and was ready to work again, I did just that. Not so much for financial reasons—I had three or four months' worth of savings—as for the principle: I wanted to make my ex-boss pay, even in some small way, for what she'd done to me.

As I'd feared, she made good on her threat to contest. The unemployment office sent me a form asking for additional information about my decision to quit my job. Unbeknownst to my ex-boss, I'd been quietly documenting everything from work hours to incidents of verbal abuse in emails to my doctor for almost a year before I quit, and I was able to give specific details — dates and times — of conversations I'd had, with her and with my doctor, about my health issues. I also gave details of how my bullying boss's mistreatment had harmed my health: "...feelings of sadness and hopelessness, irritability, sleep disturbances, changes in appetite, difficulty concentrating and remembering — and, at the end of my employment with the company, crying before, during, and after work, and thoughts of death as my only way out...Frequent interruptions and distractions made it difficult for me to concentrate, or to complete tasks. Excessive overtime contributed to my sleep difficulties. My condition requires a consistent sleep schedule for optimal stability... [My employer's] management style...included verbal abuse, manipulation, and threats."

One week after my response, I received an email informing me that the decision on my unemployment benefits would be made that day. The next day, the decision came to me via letter: "... benefits are allowed." By then it was January 6: in the Christian tradition, the feast of the Epiphany. I'd already had one epiphany in November, that there was a whole world out there away from the verbal abuse, manipulation, and threats. Now I had another: that I could stand up to someone who intimidated me and win, even when the odds were not in my favor.

I found myself thinking of my father, who beat Stage IV lung cancer back into remission and lived seven years with a diagnosis that had been expected to kill him in less than one. He, too, had fought something frightening, against overwhelming odds. That third epiphany, that I'd inherited something of Dad's fighting spirit, made me smile. Six months before he died, he'd made me promise I would make taking care of myself my number-one priority, since he wouldn't be around anymore to make sure I did. I realized that though he may not have been with me physically, Dad had been right behind me in spirit.

FOUR PIECES OF ADVICE:

1. Document EVERYTHING–dates, times, and (if any) witnesses of incidents.
2. Do NOT let the perps know you've been documenting the bullying. They will be blindsided by your next move–a complaint to HR, a resignation, or even an EEOC claim or lawsuit–and that's what you want. Don't give them the time or ammunition to respond.

3. Do whatever you have to do to take care of yourself, whether that means staying and trying to change things, looking for a new job, or quitting without a new job lined up.
4. Get support wherever you can: a doctor, counselor, support group, friends and/or family.

Marisa Wood is a former HR specialist living in the Pacific Northwest. Her story is a case in point for why HR may not be your first line of defense against workplace bullying. When human resources staff do care and want to help, they may have their hands tied by upper management or may be targets themselves.

FOUR

JUST BE AWESOME
Anonymous

As a "related arts" teacher, I do not teach a subject that is considered "important" by many. My subject is not tested; therefore, no data is collected about my students' work (or my impact as a teacher). My subject isn't considered a real subject, by most administrators, even though I am held to the same requirements by state law as any other teacher. I am to instruct my students and ensure they learn according to the state educational standards.

Teachers do not really respect arts teachers, and we are seen as babysitters to watch the kids during their planning time. Even though I have twice the educational credentials as many teachers, they would often try to bully me. For instance, since I had to travel from room to room, it was almost impossible to adhere to a schedule 100% of the time, especially since travel time was not included in scheduling. One teacher would routinely call the office to complain if I was a minute or two late, regardless of the reason. Then, she would return 5-10 minutes late from her planning time, which would cut that amount out of my lunch break. Another teacher rallied all the other teachers to raise hell about my getting an extra planning period one day a week (that I usually spent doing other work for the school anyway) and got the administration to give me an extra class. Teachers will go into my classroom to "borrow" supplies on days I am not even in the building, and since the room is used for other things on those days, my room is always unlocked.

Administrators are bullies, too. Since they are ultimately in charge of making schedules, and since arts classes do not have minimum time requirements, administrators can give us as much or as little time with students as they want to. State guidelines recommend that traveling teachers be given travel time when they have to move from class to class, but they aren't required to. They are required by law to give us planning time, but one principal gave me planning time before school even started, and there wasn't much I could do about it. And when I complained about any of this, most principals simply said they couldn't do anything to help me because they had other requirements to meet. Some principals would even retaliate by giving me an even worse schedule the next year, or negative marks on my evaluations.

I thought about quitting teaching, but I really love making art with kids, so I didn't do that. I did stop doing all the "extras" (murals, bulletin boards, t-shirt designs, etc...) for the schools that treated me badly and just did my job as best I could every day. I put all my energy into my students and really just stopped giving a fig about the teachers and administrators who tried to bully me. I didn't allow them to have any of my energy — it's too precious and they're not why I'm here anyway. I worked my way into three schools that could give me support and reasonable scheduling, and an actual classroom. I am not completely free of bullying, but I do stand up for myself. I kind of have a reputation of being difficult, but I don't even care. I am going back to school to get my Master's degree and I am working toward finding more ways to advocate for stronger arts programs in schools. Along the way, I have picked up some pretty impressive awards. I've developed my resume, and I've made a name for myself, despite the bullying and the drama. I did what I could to develop myself professionally so I could move out of those schools and into better opportunities. I think that spending time getting awards, grants, and professional development for myself was sort of my therapy. The good feelings I got from those development experiences went a long way towards countering the bad feelings from the bullying. I felt like I had a secret identity that the bullies didn't get to see.

I also got a lot of support from other teachers who I looked up to. I found that a lot of the most amazing teachers are often the target of bullies because they make lazy teachers look bad. I learned lots of coping mechanisms from them. They helped me to remain excited about the things that make me love teaching and let the other things go. I also got a lot of support from my family, especially my husband and my Mom who are both passionate teachers. Lastly, I spend as much time as I can doing things that make me feel alive — travel, art, getting outdoors — and giving me something to do besides stressing about work drama.

Looking back, I wish that I had known my rights as a teacher. It's hard to advocate for your rights if you don't know what they are. I also wish I had understood that the reasons teachers and administrators are such bullies is because there is so much pressure, so little funding, and so much focus on completely unrealistic (and meaningless) goals, with so many real problems being completely ignored. These people are desperate to do their jobs (as they see them) that they will throw anyone under the proverbial bus to get their gold star.

I also wish that I had put more effort into self-care instead of beating myself up over perceived failures and feeling sad about mean people. It's much better to go kayaking and enjoy the misty morning air over a beautiful lake than to spend time feeling sorry for myself.

I wish that I had put more time and effort into professional development (I hate that phrase... it sounds so boring, but it's so important to develop your practice for real, not just sit in some seminars, passively) and surrounding myself with people who do amazing things early on. That has been the biggest factor in getting over bullying. When you're awesome at what you do, it shows, even when bullies are trying to detract from it. People will respect you, and will stand up for you when bullies try to mess with you. The bullies tend to look pretty stupid when they try to push you around and you're the star player on your team.

To anyone experiencing workplace bullying, I recommend that you just do everything you can to be awesome at what you do. Get that degree or certification. Apply for fellowships. Go to that conference. Surround yourself with people who are doing awesome things, and who will energize you about what made you want to follow this path to begin with. Educate yourself about your rights, but also learn as much as you can about what you do. Be THE authority on what you do. Remember that bullies often feel powerless, and are looking for the easiest way to escape negative consequences themselves, so they shuffle their issues off onto other people. Be so awesome that they look stupid when they try to blame you for anything. Stay connected to things you're passionate about, whether they have anything to do with your job or not — these are the things that make it worth getting out of bed in the morning. And most of all, don't give any of your precious time and energy to people who are just trying to make you look bad or dump their problems off onto you. "No" is a complete sentence. If you have to find another job and move on to escape bullying, it is entirely worth it.

FIVE PIECES OF ADVICE:

1. Know your rights and be able to cite them at any time. Carry reference materials if you need to. (Seriously, I laminated the policy I needed and carried it with me everywhere.)
2. Refuse to accept anything less than what's fair. Ever. Don't be afraid to report it, even if all you get out of it is documentation.
3. You gotta fight... for your rights... for EVERYTHING. Join a union or professional organization that will help you in this fight. Band with other employees who get the same treatment, if for no other reason than commiseration (but hopefully you can work together to solve it).
4. If it doesn't get better, leave. No job is worth being treated unfairly.
5. Draw attention to injustice, don't hide it. You may help someone who thinks there is no hope.

FIVE

STAY
Benjamin

I t was during her welcoming party that the newly hired Assistant Director of Human Resources sidled up to me and after looking around in conspiratorial fashion, asked me in a whisper, "Why do you stay?" The question, something I'd asked myself on countless other occasions, threw me for a loop even though I'd thought about it numerous times. I just wasn't prepared for it, coming from a new managerial employee like it just had. One thing was for sure, I told myself; she's only been here a few days and she's already seen my file. It was the only reason for such a query; it had to be, I thought at the time. I mean, why else would you ask such a question, seemingly chastising a valued colleague for his at the time 12 years of dedicated service under some very extreme circumstances? That she was aware of the checkered history I and the company shared was very apparent. But if I figured that her supposed knowledge of past unfair transgressions against me perpetrated by the company were finally to be addressed then I had another thing coming.

Fifteen years ago, I answered an ad for a shipping clerk in an internationally renowned non-profit cancer research association. During my interview, much was made about my temperament and my being able to "coexist" with a combative employee. I was told that I would be working with a gentleman who was bombastic and challenging and that it would be imperative that I maintained a level head on my shoulders and not respond to any aggression. I assured the then Assistant Director of HR – not the one 12 years later with the probing question-that not only was there no record in my personal life of any violence, there existed none in my business life either.

Bells should've gone off in my head and I should've walked away from the possible position. But I needed a job desperately, both kids were still at home, I was in between positions and my unemployment had run out, extensions and all. The wolves were circling, so to speak.

So began my journey into the dark world of workplace bullying. I'd never heard of it but after the first time my co-worker ran across the room and got all up in my face, I knew then that I wasn't in any type of ordinary workplace situation. Most importantly, I also knew that keeping this particular job was going to be difficult. Imagine going to work daily, not knowing what type of mood your coworker is going to be in or just how far he would go today. Is this the day I really have to protect myself? Now add to the mix the fact that his immediate supervisor, our boss and the one who hired me and who I expect to protect me from abuse, was afraid of him. Imagine that for a minute. It soon became clear that she wasn't the only one; many others in the company were as well. After a few months, I was pegged to be the sacrificial lamb, the scapegoat. Managers saw that while I wasn't violent, I also wasn't going to let anyone hurt me either. I was given a final warning during my first review with the company because of my inability to work peacefully with my coworker. The message was clear; I was about to be fired during my probationary period. Having done nothing wrong, I decided to fight whatever was about to happen, so I brought charges of an unfair workplace to my state's Human Relations Commission. And I won. There was no monetary award, simply the right to work in an atmosphere free from verbal or emotional abuse. Unfortunately, that wasn't to be. If anything, the behavior of my colleague didn't change and a stranger thing happened. I began to sense the company, or certain senior employees, feeling a certain way about me. I was denied advancement (it took me ten years to get a promotion), denied raises, and denied the benefit of training even though I watched and listened as other employees, some newly arriving, throughout the company reaped the rewards of such benefits.

It was about this time that I discovered Dr. Namie and the Bullybusters at WBC. I have no problem saying that before I happened on the website, there were nights when I didn't know how I was going to go to work the next day. In no uncertain terms, Dr. Namie gave me the strength to do that. He made me realize first and foremost that it wasn't me, nor was it others out there like me. It wasn't our fault. I think it was that recognition of the existence of this national phenomenon that fortified me the most. It helped me in making my decision of whether to quit my job or stay. I decided to stay, and fight.

Fight is an ugly word, a violent one that in no way depicts what I had in mind. My plan simply was not to give them what I knew they wanted, aka my resignation. Instead, I began to communicate what I felt was happening to Human Resources. This however brought no change, no relief. So I upped the ante and wrote my association's entire Board of Directors telling them of the past years of abuse I'd suffered. That brought results. Again, not the relief I anticipated, just more intense scrutiny. The problem is that my company, even today, feels they are above reproach. I know this now and can truthfully say it. In my letter, I told the Board that the situation I was suffering through was created solely by HR and that it was their dereliction of duty that allowed my suffering to continue all these years. I further added that it was only because both parties, I and my coworker, were black that allowed such indolence on the part of HR. I closed by saying that if either of us was of a different class, they would have had to take some sort of action by now. I remember the day Board members got their letters because that's the day I got the evil eye from many of the company's most senior employees including the CEO. My name was mud and it would be from that point on. But that was OK because by then I had figured out why I was still there.

I realized I was still there because I was good at what I did; I had to be in order to work there. With the help of Dr.Namie and the WBC, I felt empowered to make my own decision about whether I quit or whether I stayed, knowing full well that if I stayed, there would be some hell to pay somedays. I found out years later that it's called Job Embeddedness; where people stay at jobs they don't necessarily like for reasons of their own.

Today, after 15 years and only one promotion, I'm comfortable with my decision back then. It came from a place of wanting to show how wrong people were about me personally and about black men in particular. Oh yes, there was a racial component that the length of this doesn't lend me time to describe. It came from a place that wanted to illustrate how we use our minds to combat injustice and not our fists; where we use our words as weapons to fight tyranny. Earlier this year during a low period that I occasionally get, I wrote a piece and posted it on the webpage www.

<u>Glassdoor.com</u>. At work, the querying HR AD came to my cubicle with the same conspiratorial tone and asked if I'd seen the post on Glassdoor, saying she was sure it came from "over here." I told her I didn't know what she was talking about.

She went on to say that it made no difference since the post had been taken down. I knew that; I chickened out. What's the use of bitching like that? If I've discovered anything in the 15 years of working in such an environment it's that, **you want to win** and you don't win by fouling your mood. For me, winning was staying and fighting, with the help of a loving family and an occasional trip to the WBC page. There comes a time when you have to treat a workplace bully just like an ordinary bully down the block. Smack the workplace bully in the mouth with your hard work, dedication and the subsequent success it creates, however little that success is. Even as the job itself becomes the bully personified, your commitment to service will always win out. Besides, I'm trying to outlast them all.

Company scuttlebutt has it that if you get on the CEO's bad side, you might as well resign. In that way, they continue their bad habits. On the other hand, I think I've grown; at least enough to make it through to my 20-year mark and retire. It's about me after all. And that's something else I got from Dr. Namie.

FIVE PIECES OF ADVICE:

1. Relationships will be important. Even if you leave, a support system of some sort works wonders during those low points. And in the world of workplace bullying, handling low points is key to physical and emotional survival. Remember, stress kills.
2. Don't be afraid to communicate your concerns to your manager, HR and above, as you see fit. Follow your organizational chart; be respectful but be unwavering.
3. Did I say there'd be low points? Don't be afraid to cry; you too, men. Frustration is a powerful emotion and should be vented. Don't bring it home; you know what I mean. Connect with other sufferer's on Bullybusters.
4. Know your rights. Find out if you're in a class where litigation is possible. Talk to your state Human Relations Commission or Civil Rights Division. If necessary, go to the EEOC (Equal Employment Opportunities Commission). In this case, knowledge is truly power.
5. Realize you are the injured party. It unties your hands and makes action possible.

Ben is still with the company in Philadelphia, serving as an Operations Department Coordinator. He's a free-lance writer, blogger and gardener who's written numerous garden articles for Examiner.com. You can connect with him on one of his blogs: **I'm Just Saying** *at* https://benderedondat.wordpress.com *and* **The Displaced Farmer** *at* https://urbanvegetablesoldier.wordpress.com

SIX

HAPPY ME
Anonymous

I was teaching as an ESP (Education Support Professional) at a place for approximately one year. In the beginning, things seemed to be going very well, or so I thought. The entire second half of the year things were just not adding up. The administration started having me do things out of my grade level, and not letting me have any contact with the students I had been teaching for the entire first half of the year. The administration began the bullying with name calling and excluding me from school activities. I sought out the advice of the school union rep. They told me that this treatment was common-place. I went to a field representative (luckily I had paperwork to document my claim). After speaking to the field representative I decided to file a grievance with the administration – (which I WON – and I'm so glad I did! The action I took has me in the place I am now IN – "Happy Me! Since filing my grievance, the principal of that school received a vote of NO CONFIDENCE – and was removed from the school.

I learned that it comes to this: Listen To – and USE YOUR INSTINCTS – That's why you've GOT them! If things are NOT adding up for you, DOCUMENT EVERYTHING (time, date, place and parties involved). Believe in your abilities; remember you CHOSE your field and you wouldn't have CHOSEN it – if you didn't TRULY LOVE what you do. Seek advice from your building representatives. Seek support from your field representatives out there; they are there to give you the CONFIDENCE you will need to successfully navigate your way through the experience. Finally, pay attention to your work environment; you can inspire others as well by the standards YOU set NOW. We are giving hope, inspiration, and courage to do the right thing because whatever the right thing IS for you, you will be a stronger person FOR it. Dr. Martin Luther King Jr. said it best: „The time is ALWAYS right to do what is right."

FIVE PIECES OF ADVICE:

1. Pay attention to your work environment.
2. If things do NOT add up in your work environment, get advice from your building delegate or field representative.
3. DOCUMENT EVERYTHING (time, date(s), place, and parties involved.

4. BELIEVE IN YOUR CAPABILITIES AND YOURSELF – ALWAYS!
5. Use your professionalism, positivity and courage to inspire those who will learn from the legacy we create in the present, to build upon for years to come.

SEVEN

FIVE TOOLS THAT HELPED ME
SURVIVE A WORKPLACE BULLY
Monique Caissie

W hen I watched the powerful 2012 documentary called "Bullied," I cried in recognition, grief, anger, and sheer sense of helplessness to stop it. At the end, there were memorials for children who had taken their lives because of bullying. I wanted to reach through my TV and shake those school principals and parents. I understood the victims and their sense of isolation and despair. The main difference between children's bullying and adults' bullying is that the more "mature" bully leaves no physical scars. After all, there are laws for that! Having worked in mental health, I've seen the other kinds of scars. Unfortunately, I've also been victim to them myself.

Years ago, I worked at a children's charity. The Executive Director (ED) verbally abused staff. The first time I heard her scream, I thought she was injured and ran into her office. I was shocked when I realized screaming was her way of asking for a file. I was expected to intuitively predict her needs or incur her wrath. Charming!

She looked like somebody's Grandma, complete with stuffed toys in her office and cross-stitched frames with statements of kindness and love. Actually, if you are familiar with Harry Potter, she was like Dolores Umbridge with her kitten plates, except her eyes bulged more.

This ED was revered in the community and at her church as a do-gooder. When people would come to the office to discuss making a donation, she would tearfully gush about how wonderful they were to support the children. After they left, she would call them the most ungodly names saying they were (insert bad word here) cheap.

"Knowing what's right doesn't mean much unless you do what's right." Theodore Roosevelt

WHY BULLY?

According to the Workplace Bullying Institute, bullies are more likely to intimidate and discredit the stronger, more competent people and not the ones who are weaker. Their targets also have different values from their own: including ethics, integrity, fairness, and collaborativeness. The payback for bullying is that by discrediting their colleague/subordinate, the bully's career usually thrives. This was most certainly my ED's case.

I didn't leave right away. I stayed because I loved the cause, got along great with my colleagues and was fearful of being unemployed again.

If you're in that very difficult situation, here's your toolbox:

TOOL # 1

Learn how to speak up. First I asked her to please tell me what she wanted or needed, "one thing at a time." Her response was to look at me with disgust and question my intelligence. I repeated that I needed her to be clearer and to remain respectful so that I could help her. The other thing I did was to firmly say, "Please do not shout." She was shocked that someone would tell her "not to shout." When she couldn't deny what had just happened, she would dramatically grab her chest and say that she is a breast cancer survivor from 15 years ago. Then she would whimper that this was "affecting her today."

When I spoke up, there were times that she would stop for a while; but she had more experience and endurance at bullying than I did at stopping her. Still, my small successes gave me a temporary sense of control. Bullies need silence to continue their bullying.

TOOL # 2

Find out the history of the company and who might help. During my interview, I questioned the high turnover of that position. They explained that non-profits can't pay well enough to keep people. That was a red herring. It quickly became apparent that she had a long history of bullying. Long-time bullies ALWAYS have people protecting them and making excuses.

One of the board members, who originally interviewed me, told me that it is the fault of the employees for tolerating the behaviors and for staying. I pointed out to her that "nobody stays." Out of curiosity, I asked this board member what was great about this ED. It turns out that she had helped them get rid of a "bad" Director who was destroying their reputation and ability to raise money. They felt "forever in her debt." It was clear that no one was going to help the staff. Basically, the ED knew where the body was buried. When they start blaming the victim, as this board member did with me: GET OUT! The cost of staying is too high.

TOOL # 3

Learn your legal rights. It's hard to take action when you fear retaliation. Because of that same inaction, victims of bullying may have rights they are unaware of. In my case, I believed that if I quit, I would not be eligible for unemployment benefits and I needed an income while looking for another job. Clearly, this woman would not give a fair work reference so I felt fearful and stuck.

When my father unexpectedly died, her abuse escalated. I quit and reported her to my provincial Labour Standards with documented events. It turned out there was already a file on her from past victims and I received benefits right away. So check out free legal clinics and get informed.

Two years later, my successor called me saying she had found the detailed letter of resignation I had written to the board. She wanted to thank me for validating her experience. Until she read my letter to her husband, he thought she was making stuff up. I mean come on: that sweet Grandma, devoting her life to a children's charity – a bully? No way! She quit after we spoke and, following my recommendations, she also received all her benefits.

TOOL #4

After leaving a serious bullying situation, take some time to heal! THIS IS IMPORTANT! Recovery from bullying takes time. Just switching jobs without getting emotionally grounded could be a recipe for disaster. Having worked as a crisis counsellor, I can tell you that there is nothing brave about ignoring your mental health. Don't play with fire – put some emotional distance, catch your breath and heal. Do not wait for a diagnosis of a burnout, depression or anxiety disorder. You'll transition better into a new job and increase your future successes.

TOOL # 5

Helping others can empower you. The last time I was bullied at a job, I had learned from the ED experience above. This last time, I quickly recognized the signs and I was very capable of protecting my well-being and helping other targets. Although I am no longer there, I know that I made a difference for my colleagues by supporting and guiding them. I was able to stay calm while properly alerting her superiors to her specific behaviours. Because I was calm and detailed, instead of emotional like my colleagues, people took notice. I eventually left for greener pastures, but, even after I left, she couldn't burp without the hierarchy taking notice. When she finally left and to this day, my old colleagues remain beyond thrilled. Be a survivor – not a victim.

TWO HAVENS FOR BULLIES

A therapist I used to work with told me she could build an entire practice treating people who are victims of bullies in non-profits and churches. We have an identity attachment to our religious life or when we pick a job in support of a passionate cause. Because of the helping and/or forgiving environment fostered in these environments, calculating bullies can get away with a lot.

My life choices mean I was in both of these havens. I'm still sad when I think of the abuse I went through in a toxic church. I was cyber-bullied and treated very unfairly by one person in particular. I was told by others that even though she invited me to help out, "She is quite territorial." Just like the board protected the ED in the story above, the pastor protected the bully in this church. One witness, who has also left this church, described the way I was treated as "being unjustly crucified."

Emotionally, I know what she meant. Here's the baseline to look for in a healthy environment: There should be space to have a voice and feel respected or move on! Do you know how to speak up? Or do you avoid those difficult conversations? Get my free four-step cheat sheet on asking for what you want. You won't regret it. Here's the link: http://bit.ly/2askpage

FIVE PIECES OF ADVICE:

1. Learn how to speak up.
2. Find out the history of the company and who might help.
3. Learn your legal rights.
4. After leaving a serious bullying situation, take some time to heal!
5. Helping others can empower you.

Monique's strategies to empower others to stand up and take control of their personal and professional lives are appreciated by all who meet her. Her goal is to teach others to have better conversations with people who "drive them crazy!"

As a speaker, facilitator, consultant and coach, helping to reduce conflict and increase collaboration, Monique draws from 30 years of crisis intervention and counselling work to help others increase their confidence to feel more heard, respected and happier.

She is an Accredited Trainer for DISC as a Human Behavior Consultant and a Certified NLP Professional Coach. She is a regular contributor to Huffington Post. She is also easily found on her website by her name or on Linked In.

EIGHT

FRENZY: A TRUE TALE OF MOBBING AND RECOVERY

C. Goodison

I teach at one of the country's largest public universities. My career began ten years ago. When I entered the profession, I approached my job with a great deal of enthusiasm and idealism. My personal experience with college life was mostly positive. I wanted to share some of that joy through learning with my students, nearly all of whom were like me: ambitious, practical children of immigrants. These were working class people like me, and they knew what it meant to struggle. I wanted to give them all that I could. I didn't want them to leave college feeling they were shortchanged or had missed out on opportunity. I threw myself into my work and put in long hours. I expected nothing. I felt truly honored to be in the position that I was, and I enjoyed my students. They possessed a sincerity and drive that

I admired and found inspiring. In a few words, I loved my job.

I sensed trouble on the first day of work but thought nothing of it. I'd entered a politicized workplace that seemed divided on the bases of age, gender and race. There was a clear generation gap born of hiring freezes and this, I believed, partly explained some of the divisions. I later realized it was more complicated than that. It was simply a dysfunctional workplace where a few longer-serving faculty who had been mistreated were eager to pass on some of that mistreatment. There were cliques and there were many lingering resentments. It never occurred to me that doing my job well and finding great joy in it would make me a target for abuse.

Two years after I began, our department selected a department chair to replace our old one who suddenly retired. I and the two other women I was hired with were very nervous about this change because this new chairperson had made it clear from the beginning that she hated us. Why? It was not clear. The feminist in me wants to say it was not petty jealousy and insecurity, but no other answer presents itself. The women who I was hired with were highly competent and very talented people, in addition to being beautiful people. They had the kind of beauty born of self-assurance, with an easy confidence engaging with the whole wide world. One of the women quit not long after our leadership changed; the other was able to find reassignments inside and outside of the department. I became a target. My outspokenness about bullying didn't help.

My troubles began as soon as my new chairperson took over. There were whispering campaigns to the "higher-ups" in the administration and among the more senior faculty within my department that I was actually not the nice person everyone thought I was. These people who would be asked to make decisions on my reappointment, my tenure (if I ever got there) and my promotions (if I were lucky!) were being fed a great deal of misinformation. There were many rumors, all of it behind closed doors, where I was not able to defend myself, and pretty soon I was a pariah. No one wanted to talk to me.

I started to receive negative (I would say defamatory) evaluations that were contrary to the truth. Friends and family reported to me that all sorts of things were being posted about me online — things that were meant to question my character and my abilities as a teacher. I later learned that this was standard treatment for all of the college's scapegoats—mostly blacks, women, the foreign-born, gay, or anyone deemed "too nice," (i.e. popular). I would get supposedly professional emails addressed to "Bootylicious." I had porn pinned to my door. I received anonymous mail telling me why I need to quit. My chairperson called me into her office so she could scream in my ear, "Nobody likes you!!" Or, that "You never do what you're supposed to do!!" I would ask for specifics but none were forthcoming. She'd roll her neck and eyes and gurgle something like it didn't matter. It was like these charges weren't supposed to mean anything, despite the screaming and the rage.

It got worse. I would be at home working on Thanksgiving weekend and receive a letter by courier saying I had been non-reappointed. There were never any explanations. What this meant was I had to suspend my professional duties — my life — in order to write pleading letters for various committees where I was asked to appear, during my Christmas break, so I could be accused of things I didn't do by people who had formed an opinion of me based on one person's lies. This happened every year for four or five years and never once got easier. Human Resources and the college administration joined with my bully. They were afraid to intervene. They needed the chairpersons and the bully chairpersons formed a tight unit. It wasn't worth the fuss of their sabotaging their own positions for the sake of one or two employees.

I became very ill — It's not over and I'm still in recovery for PTSD and a host of physical ailments brought on by stress. I felt very isolated. It's like I had a contagious disease and no one wanted to catch it. My home life suffered as the stress of the situation became too much for my partner and myself. I sought the help of my union. I was very lucky. They're one of the good ones and I found real advocates among them. They fought for me. They kept my spirits up. They offered community and support. They provided me with information on bullying and on the particular dynamics of my workplace. They gave me understanding of the situation so I could stop blaming myself for getting sick, for crying every day, and for struggling at work. They helped rectify the abuses, won me redress, and changed the workplace by challenging the bigotry and cruelty rampant throughout the college culture. I owe them my life. Where am I now? I'm pursuing a spiritual path, one that provides me with much nourishment and wisdom. I am a devout Buddhist and Episcopalian. What advice do I have for others now suffering from workplace bullying? I honestly don't know, because when you are in the middle of it, all you can think about is your survival. Some of us don't make it. There are suicides... I understand how someone could give up and take his or her life. I do. I ate. Binged. That's all I could do as I faced this toxic sludge of a workplace every single day.

Some people run, whether literally or metaphorically. My point is I don't think I can honestly give anyone advice knowing what I know about the hell of this experience. I say, try to get some distance from it. Leave if you can. Leave if you can't. Maybe there is sick leave. Maybe there is leave without pay. But leave. Stay with friends and relatives. Tell them you need a few weeks (you'll likely need more but you've got to start somewhere) in order to decompress and practice some self-care. Do that. Be gentle with yourself even though you might hate yourself almost as much as you hate the sociopaths who drove you to this state. Practice radical self-care; seek out a therapist, counselor, a wise friend. Find a supportive community: A sangha, a church, a recovery group. Find people who you can be yourself with; those with whom you can cry and be sad and who won't judge you.

Get a dog. Get a cat. Get a plant. Get a living thing that you can trust and that can show you how to rest and how to ask for what you need and how to be vulnerable and how to grow. Read uplifting books. Call a friend. Road trip! Tune out anything that doesn't nourish you. Go on retreat, or do as I did and take up residence in monasteries. It's not obvious now, but one day it will be. There are a lot of damaged people in the world, and you've been turned into one of them. But because you've worked so hard and because you've allowed yourself to be human, to feel and to cry and to be sad, you've heard your heart's wisdom and you know that you have the choice, the freedom to not traumatize in return (not yourself or anyone else) but to use your story to heal others. You can only help others after you've healed yourself. That's the caveat. You're a great gift for the universe, and you've got in touch with your true nature, which is to help others, but you've got to do everything to care for you first. Step one. Get some distance. Leave.

THREE PIECES OF ADVICE:

1. Take sick leave if you can / retreat.
2. Find a supportive spiritual community.
3. Practice radical self-care.

C. Goodison is a professor and author.

NINE

CAUGHT WITH LOVING ARMS
Sarah Callus

After seven years in my job as a manager in the student accommodation sector, I was yearning a new challenge, a change. One day on my way home from work, I drove past a new student accommodation building that was being built. How had I not seen that before?! There was a big banner on the front of the scaffolding with an email address and telephone number. As soon as I got home I sent an email enquiring if there were any jobs available. A few days later I received a response and an email inviting me to meet the Director the following week. Apparently she was interested and wanted to talk to me about potential opportunities! Yeeha! At last, maybe this was my ticket out?

A week later I met her at a hotel in town. She was about fifty, dressed in skinny jeans and a white shirt and I remember thinking how cool she looked. We sat and chatted and there and then she offered me a job in Manchester. "Are you up for an adventure?" she asked me. She had already appointed a Manager for the site I had seen in town so this was the next best thing. I would get the new building up and running for about six months and then manage a scheme in Bristol. I love Bristol! I'd been looking at jobs in Bristol! I went home and thought about it, talked to friends and family and to be honest, I couldn't turn it down. It was handed to me on a glittery, shimmering, silver platter. The salary was fantastic, the company provided me with a penthouse apartment free of charge so I wouldn't have to rent out my own home while I was away.

You know what they say about things being too good to be true? Well this is exactly how this situation turned out to be. Rose tinted glasses on, clueless, unaware of the horrors that lay ahead; just like Snow White.

In July 2012, I packed up my belongings, squeezed them into my Fiat 500 and set off up the M50. I went straight to the new building to have a look. It was very impressive, all thirty-five floors of it. All brand new, modern, high tech, appealing, shiny, just like the juicy apple; tempting me in, mesmerizing. The penthouse was impressive too and all mine for the foreseeable future. I had made it; I had done so well whispered my little ego. The first few weeks lulled me into a false sense of security. Myself and the new team spent our days in an adjoining office, getting ready for opening and trying to get organized. It was fun, it was new, it felt good. In September, just a day before over five hundred students arrived, we moved into our gorgeous, pristine new building. Then things went downhill rapido! Long hours, working till 10 pm, working weekends, dealing with emergencies, floods, water pouring through light fittings and power sockets, getting called in on my days off, manipulative staff and bosses, back stabbing, spying, negativity.

My bubble was burst and my glorious illusion was shattered. It wasn't long before I started thinking I don't want this. Oh, what had I done? I'd gone from my easy, boring job to this hell! And the fun had only just started!

After nine months in Manchester, it was time for me to return home and start thinking about the Bristol scheme. Boy was I ready! I had had enough of the job in Manchester and all the negativity and stress that came with it. I was promoted to Regional Manager and I was responsible for the property in Bristol and Cardiff. The Director had become increasingly impatient with the Manager at the Cardiff scheme and wanted me to be more involved. I divided my time between the two cities but I couldn't do right for doing wrong. When I was in Cardiff I was wanted back in Bristol, when I was in Bristol I should have been Cardiff. When I was in Cardiff, certain manipulative members of staff in Bristol, who were in the Directors' favor, spread lies and caused mistrust and confusion about me. It was awful. I dreaded going to work and it went from bad to worse. I was constantly being criticized for not showing any commitment, despite working long hours and weekends. Everything I did was wrong and I could feel the pressure building and the odds stacking against me. There were secret phone conversations, whispers in corridors, blatant bullying, detrimental text messages and then the final straw, the final nail in the coffin, my coffin!

On a Thursday morning in October I caught the train to Bristol as usual. During the journey, I received another text message from the Director telling me to work another weekend as one of her lap dogs needed a break! When I got to the office, one of my colleagues, a lovely man who had been on the receiving end of this company's negativity, took me aside and advised me to start looking for another job. He told me that everyone was talking about me and all the details of their poison and bitter behavior spilled out. I burst out crying (in private). My soul was dying. It was literally shriveling up. I couldn't take much more of this. I was a good person, a hard worker; this was unjustified and I didn't deserve it. Most importantly, I didn't want this anymore! I couldn't believe things had turned out this way.

I sat at my desk and saw an email from the Director full of complaints and criticisms about my performance. With it came a tsunami of demands, requests, emails from her and other departments and that's when the voice in my head and my heart said NO MORE!

I got up from my desk, grabbed my coat and bag and walked out. Yep, that's right. I walked out, jumped in a taxi, went to the train station and went home. I cried all the way, hot, relentless, pitiful tears, in full view of everyone on the busy train. I pivoted from feelings of elation, freedom, to sheer panic. My ego shrieked in disbelief, "What on earth have you done?" The universe said, "Well done child, now trust that you are on the right path. Things are exactly as they should be."

The first thing I did when I got home was phone a psychic. She told me not to worry, that I would be caught with loving arms and indeed I was. What did I learn from that experience? What I learnt was quite a revelation. I had been bullied all my life in one way or another. I had been the victim of bullying from parents, school friends, boyfriends, a husband and female bosses. I had never had a voice, I had never been able to stand up for myself and what I wanted, or voice what was important to me. I gave in to what others wanted me to do. I wouldn't say anything for fear of rocking the boat. I shrank away, and this is all about self-love isn't it? I found it difficult to be assertive but this is the area I was being tested in. I wasn't loving myself. I wasn't protecting the child that I was from parents who wanted their own way and didn't take into account what I wanted or how I felt. I wasn't protecting myself from the bosses who berated me by telling them their behavior was unacceptable.

Some people will say I didn't deal with the situation, that I ran away. In a way, I agree. By not dealing with the bullying head on, I would have to face another situation in which I was bullied. Until you learn your lesson, until you break the cycle, you will face the same problems and have to deal with the same people. However, I also see removing myself from that negative situation as an act of self-love. Isn't that where it all starts? Isn't that what lies at the heart of most of our problems? Love yourself and watch others love you back.

As I look back at that horrible chapter in my life, I can see how I was protected and guided and I'm still here to tell the tale. If I've learnt one thing, it's to trust. Trust that the universe will have your back, trust that you will emerge not without skirmishes, not without scars but that you will emerge stronger, polished, more confident, more secure in the knowledge that no matter what happens, you will always be ok, you will always get through the wars, the fire, the flames, the bed of nails, the battles.

FIVE PIECES OF ADVICE:

1. Share your experience with others, don't deal with it alone.
2. Ask yourself: Is there a senior person you can go to?
3. Ask yourself: Is this a pattern? What are you being taught?

4. Be brave, stand up for yourself.
5. Say this is not acceptable or leave if possible.

Having left her negative place of employment, Sarah went on a journey of discovery and is now a teacher and published author. Her stories are based on her real life experiences, usually challenging ones and she shares them to bring a little hope to readers, to shine a light in their own darkness.

She has written two short stories, "The Girl in the Cardboard Box," and, "Broken," and a collection of her own poems called "No Voice."

Caught with loving arms was inspired by "The Girl in the Cardboard Box," a story of Sarah's own experiences of workplace bullying.

"Know that no matter what you are experiencing at the moment, however bad it seems, you WILL get through it. You are stronger than you think and more powerful than you ever thought possible."

TEN

Healing a Broken Heart - Recovering from the Injury of Mobbing
Lorraine Segal

I dreamed I was back at the college where I worked as a professor for 20 years. In the dream, our offices were dorm rooms. I woke up suddenly in the middle of the night and knew two things — the building was on fire, and I was the only one remaining in it. The people in charge had forgotten me when they implemented the evacuation plan.

I got out of bed and looked at the door. It was locked with a double dead bolt, no doorknob or key. Terrified, I thought, "I'm trapped; I'm going to die here." But when I put my hand up and touched the door, it opened. So did the door at the entrance to the stairwell, and the one at the bottom of the stairs. I made it safely out of the building.

Later in the dream, I met with the head of the college to complain about what had happened, and how they had abandoned me. She looked at me as if I were insane, and began to calmly and reasonably justify their actions, indicating that I was the one with the problem and that they hadn't done anything wrong.

I had this dream about six months after I left the college, and the dream accurately reflects my experiences there. I endured and survived the workplace injury called mobbing, a kind of mass bullying with participation or at least collusion by management.

When I first learned the term mobbing, after most of this abuse had already taken place, I sat in my office and sobbed for an hour, in grief at what had happened to me, and in relief that there was a name for it, and I wasn't alone.

I was a skillful and hard-working professor. I got consistently good evaluations from my students and the adjunct instructors I supervised. I always finished reports on time, chaired some committees, organized cultural events at the college, did outreach to the community, and served as a consultant to colleagues about how to serve their English as a Second Language (ESL) students. My innovations were often adopted by others, although I was rarely if ever given credit.

But in the dysfunctional stew that was this workplace, my skills, hard work and creativity themselves were threatening. Because these qualities were combined with my minority status (progressive, Jewish, lesbian) and my willingness to stand up for principles and against injustice towards other minorities, I became a target.

Although the mistreatment, with major and minor incidents, continued intermittently the entire twenty years I was there, two major episodes of mass bullying (mobbing) stand out.

In my eighth year at the college, a new Division chair made her dislike for me clear. My next evaluation came up, and even though I had tenure and stellar student evaluations, she did her best to get me fired, relying on anonymous accusations with the collusion of the rest of the evaluation team. I refused to sign off on their "findings." While no one on the campus would support me, our state faculty association paid for an attorney specializing in discrimination to assist me.

It took 18 months instead of the usual three, but I finally got a satisfactory rating for my evaluation and was able to have all the false accusations removed from my file.

The school badly needed a language laboratory. When an opportunity came to get a grant and create one, I did most of the work to write the grant, design the lab, and research hardware and software. Then I learned the system and taught it to other instructors. Everyone was quite willing for me to be responsible for this, and I doubt the lab would have become a reality without my hundreds of hours of work. But, once we had the lab, I was systematically stripped of any say in its functioning, and accused of unlawful discrimination for insisting the lab tech be required to learn the new system.

This was a particularly hurtful accusation since I was one of a tiny group of people on the campus who stood up for diversity issues and for minority employees at the college, including at one point the very individual accusing me. I submitted an appeal with 70 pages of supporting documentation; and the letter of sanction was never placed in my file, but neither did I ever receive an apology or any acknowledgement of the lies and mistakes. I never felt comfortable again being in the laboratory I had worked so hard to bring to reality.

Those experiences were the beginning of the end for me. Being constantly under assault took a devastating toll on my physical and emotional well-being. I had drawn much of my self-esteem from my work, and I was baffled and deeply wounded by the virulence of this unwarranted attack against me. The most frightening part was that the truth didn't matter, that the lack of evidence for my "crimes" didn't matter, that nothing I said or did made any difference. They hated me and were determined to find me "guilty."

I tried every practical and spiritual technique I thought of or learned about to make working at that college bearable including:

Work through and with the faculty association (union), both local and state level.

Complain to and try to work with HR.

Get therapy to help with PTSD and shift my negative beliefs and attitudes that were harming me.

Journal my pain and frustration and write loving letters to myself.

Document and keep copies of everything.

Think carefully before I said or wrote anything.

Withdraw from leadership positions so I would be a less visible target.

Pray for all the people there I was angry at, for their well-being and healing, for the willingness to let go of resentments and forgive them and myself.

Detach and surround myself with light and love.

Find other sources of spiritual strength and validation.

Get support outside of the workplace.

Seek out allies at work.

Recognize the dysfunction of many there with compassion for their pain, fear, and lack of skills.

Although many of these were helpful, I ultimately realized that no attitude shift or outer action of mine were enough to keep me safe, sane, and healthy at that job. I realized that I was staying out of fear, that I had made the college and tenure my god, my only source of security. I decided to take a huge leap of faith, to believe in an abundant universe, to believe that I had the skills and ability to create a better, still prosperous life for myself. So, I walked away. Deciding to leave, to walk away from my tenured position, was perhaps the most difficult and courageous thing I've ever done. But I left to save my life and my soul. I was starting to get physical symptoms I could no longer ignore. I firmly believe I would have gotten seriously ill if I hadn't left when I did and quite possibly never have been able to work again.

As I write this, it is 8 years since I left and I am filled with gratitude for all the blessings in my life today. Out of the ashes of those horrific experiences, I have created a new immensely satisfying career as a consultant, teacher, presenter, and coach, specializing in workplace conflict, communication and bullying issues – no coincidence there.

I have survived, I have healed, and I have created a beautiful life for myself. I even accept the value of my experiences at the college, because without them I might never have found my true life's passion for helping others learn to communicate more effectively, forgive themselves and others, and navigate conflict with more ease.

FIVE PIECES OF ADVICE:

1. Name what is happening and understand that you are not responsible for the campaign against you.
2. Find other sources of spiritual strength and validation.
3. Seek support at work and outside work.
4. Look at what you can change inside yourself and in your situation.
5. If you can't improve things, get out.

Lorraine Segal is a consultant, trainer, speaker, and certified conflict management coach. She was a tenured community college professor and middle manager for many years before she found her true passion for helping people in organizations and corporations communicate better, resolve conflicts, deal with bullying issues, and let go of resentments. The goal: to create a more harmonious and productive workplace.

About her work, Lorraine says, "I bring communication expertise, creative problem-solving, a compassionate heart and spiritual connection to shine a healing light on problems at work."

Through her business, Conflict Remedy, Lorraine creates customized presentations trainings and coaching programs for nonprofit organizations, corporations, and government agencies. She teaches these skills at Sonoma State University and writes articles and blog posts.

Contact Lorraine to request a free consultation for you or your organization or stay in touch through her newsletter.

You can connect with Lorraine at:
- *Lorraine@ConflictRemedy.com*
- *https://ConflictRemedy.com*
- *https://www.linkedin.com/in/lorrainesegal/*
- *https://twitter.com/LorraineSegal*

ELEVEN

Pow. Pow. Pow.

Anonymous

O ver the course of a school year, a student in one of my classes struggled with people skills and I struggled with his mother. My student, Darren, wanted to do well. Yet, in the world of middle school he was not the top student. The bigger pond of intermediate school was a shock for him and his mom. In addition to his poor people skills that often left his classmates rolling their eyes at him or wanting him out of their groups, Darren had two gears. First gear and fifth gear. When he disliked a grade by me or another student in class, he verbally attacked me and his classmates. Pow. Pow. Pow.

Darren's mom also exhibited the same behavior. A stream of continuous, lengthy emails came at me throughout the school year, pages and pages long. Attacking: Pow. Pow. Pow. Mom emailed constantly to complain about grades. I kept my cool and always referred her and Darren to the clear directions with details and examples. It was never enough. As many teachers know, these cases keep us up at night; it makes us extremely sad and frustrated. The bullying tactics of students and parents poisons the well. Teachers, such as myself, then become targets for other parents and students who are upset with grades. The stress and bullying piles on. All of this makes a teacher want to stop teaching. Bullying affects us mentally, emotionally, and psychologically. Tears, sorrow, and discomfort ensue.

I met with the school counselor, principal, and vice-principal to seek support and guidance for what to do regarding Darren. It was decided that the vice-principal would meet with the student on a regular basis to check in on him and encourage better behavior. Unfortunately, the vice-principal then became a target as well. He began getting complaints about how the school was run, rebuttals to his suggestions regarding how to better get along with others, and his own actions as an administrator. Darren and his mom doubled down. Pow. Pow. Pow.

The complaints from this family were never short, never kind, never polite, and never ending. Perhaps it is poor people skills, or an alpha tactic used in hopes of getting what they wanted, or a mental-emotional issue. In the end, it was bullying on their part that ruined the teacher-student relationship, relationships with classmates, and with the vice-principal. Pow. Pow. Pow. Looking back, I know my conduct and decisions were correct. I documented all discussions and emails. I did my best to reach out to the student to find common ground. I went to the school counselor and other administrators.

What got me through was being professional, not arguing back, being mindful, prayer, and seeing the bigger context. If you are going to be a teacher for long, you will face the public, a public consisting of all kinds. My advice to other teachers is to do the same. I would also encourage a change in policy at my school and in other schools as well. If a teacher comes under verbal assault and email attacks, then the student should be placed in another class. Some families are so unhealthy that nothing a teacher says, does, or models will change the circumstances nor improve the relationship. We need more administrators, politicians, and families to understand the horrible consequences of bullying. Pow. Pow. Pow.

FIVE PIECES OF ADVICE:

1. Document all in-person and email conversations with students and parents.
2. Speak with experienced colleagues to get suggestions.
3. Search online for resources, information, and professional advice.
4. Do your best not to let unhealthy people rent space in your head.
5. Follow best practices.

TWELVE

TAKE CARE OF YOURSELF
Susan

I am a single female; my bully was a female supervisor. After reading about bullying, I learned that women bully often and as a means of social ranking and work differently together than men. I worked in a school with over 160 teachers, so the administration put department heads in charge of teachers in their department. The administration was physically and administratively distant from my situation, and I hope that may be why they did nothing. There were five vice principals and one principal that changed during the 12 years of my experience.

I experienced many of the classic symptoms of bullying in the workplace: exclusion, ignoring, pitting employees against each other, stealing my things, having things thrown at me, deceit, shame, blame, criticism, intrusion, bad boundaries, shifting goals, campaigning against me, on and on. I involved a male union leader and his response was to have a meeting. He concluded that, "Now that we have cleared the air, we can start a new year." I looked at him and realized he had no clue that in-girl work bullying never stops.

As the years went on, I had to get a regional union leader involved, and we looked at workplace harassment and discrimination. I was encouraged to follow every rule and to document everything in hopes that we could file a grievance. I was told that proving a hostile workplace was difficult, that it was a broad term. We were not able to prove a hostile workplace. The district did not have a policy against workplace bullying, but had a bullying policy for students.

On several occasions, I was able to show that my department head was unprofessional and she was talked to about it. My male administrator's stance was to avoid conflict so they did not get involved. I asked often why they did not have a conference with the two of us when conflicts came up, but that never happened. I did have a female administrator say, "She is bullying you, she is teaching the new people how to treat you." She was correct, and she was only at our school for 3 years.

I experienced loss of sleep, hair loss, stomach problems, eating problems, muscle problems and my stress changed who I was with the students. I educated myself about bullying; it helped to gain perspective. It helped that other teachers saw what was happening and experienced some of it. I meditated, prayed, got away as often as I could, learned ways to respond that set boundaries and developed a plan to leave because I could get no support from the administration. I am now retired. I retired as soon as I was able.

I asked myself many times what was my lesson, was it karma, what would I do differently, what helped. I would recommend educating yourself, being prepared for an uphill battle, proving bullying is as difficult as proving innocence as a rape victim.

Do your job and do it well, the bully will work to find anything wrong. Stay calm, try not to ever be alone with the bully. Be willing to get up and leave a situation. When the bully finds you alone, say, "I am uncomfortable, may we please discuss this in the presence of a third party." Know that bullies will never change. They will never be your friend and you can't trust them. They will always change their answer to unsettle you. They are broken; it is not about you.

You may be able to survive the situation but there will be a cost, so make a plan. Identify the situation, analyze what policies are in place and what administration is willing and able to do. Ask yourself what are your options; and what is the cost to your health, relationships and well-being. Develop a support group you can debrief to, eat nutritiously, stay fit, get spiritual help and use many different exercises to let go of the negative energy that came at you. Don't let it steal from your here and now.

FIVE PIECES OF ADVICE:

1. Trust your gut that something is wrong.
2. Educate yourself about bullying.
3. Document, Document, Document.
4. Develop a support system.
5. Develop a plan.

THIRTEEN

WHEN THE WORKPLACE BULLY IS YOUR OWN SCHOOL DISTRICT
Sue Gannett

I n 2005, after 23 years as an excellent school
counselor whose primary job is handling
bullying issues, I became the victim of workplace
bullying. I reported a colleague for numerous
illegal and unethical activities. Little did I know
when you blow the whistle on illegal, unethical
practices by a co-worker who has close ties
with upper administration, it doesn't matter
how excellent an educator you are, there will be
repercussions.

Thus began my six-year battle of bullying,
harassment, and discrimination. The bully was
my school district. It was incomprehensible, after
23 years of excellent evaluations and glowing
feedback, the district would become my bullying
nightmare. I was disciplined and forced to transfer
to a school housing the Emotionally Disturbed
Program. Here, my principal scrutinized every

aspect of my job, subjecting me to overwhelming duties, job threats, inequitable and harsh treatment, humiliation in staff meetings, isolation, and constantly reminding me of the transfer and discipline issues. This abuse took a toll on my emotional and physical health, resulting in a diagnosis of PTSD from all the verbal and emotional abuse. Also, my heart condition, a mitral valve prolapse, begin to worsen.

Despite my doctor's and therapist's recommendations to alleviate my stress because of my deteriorating heart condition, the administration continued their harassment and bullying. Four months later, my cardiologist determined my heart was enlarging, and open heart surgery was necessary. Because of the seriousness of this surgery, I went to Cleveland Clinic. The bullying continued, from repeatedly asking me to schedule my open-heart surgery during the summer to attending pre-op tests on weekends so I would not disrupt school schedules. Amid my cardiologist's recommendation and over the objections of administrators, I had open heart surgery in April 2007.

The district did not cause my heart condition, but my doctors verified the emotional distress greatly exacerbated the enlargement of my heart. After a five-month recovery, I returned to work in August 2007. The excessive criticism of my work abilities and unreasonable job demands continued, but now I was also dealing with physical abuse by students in the ED program. They struck my back with their pack; kicked and bit me. Being five months post op, I feared for my physical safety. When I communicated my concerns to administrators, it fell on deaf ears, with them questioning my ability to do my job. They stated, don't be a "difficult, demanding" teacher.

To no avail, my association lawyer and cardiologist continued their objections against the school for continually putting me in harmful situations with out of control students. Four months later, I suffered a mini stroke (TIA) on the ski slope. Helplessly, my husband and two children watched as I was rushed via helicopter back to my local hospital. Here, they discovered a massive blood clot on my repaired mitral valve. Because of the precarious position and seriousness of the clot, I went on Short-term Disability along with numerous prescriptions and doctor appointments every other day. Upon returning from leave, my cardiologist and association lawyer sent a letter to the district stating the need to transfer me to a school where there wasn't such a high risk for physical injury. The district refused. Again, my association lawyer stepped in and I was transferred to my old school.

As my health slowly started to improve, I thought my bullying ordeal was over, but the district continued to bully me. The district reduced my counseling position hours which made me ineligible for medical benefits which I so desperately needed. This was a violation of my rights under the Americans with Disabilities Act. My lawyer, on my behalf, filed a discrimination/ harassment lawsuit in Federal Court against the district for violating my ADA rights. Finally in 2013 I won a settlement against the district.

Yes, it was over, but until you are a victim of this kind of bullying, it is hard to understand the unending nightmares that haunt me to this day. I could not have survived this ordeal without my heroes who include: I. My husband and two children who continued to support and love me thru all the false accusations and allegations of this ordeal and my association lawyer who offered excellent legal advice, and believed in me and the case. She encouraged, cried, and fought for me every step of the way. II. My real friends and colleagues, who stood up for me and by me, thru the false allegations and attacks on my character. I thank them all. I thank my doctors for repairing my heart and giving me a new lease on life. I also thank my therapist, who picked up all my broken emotional pieces and put them back together again.

A strong support system is essential to surviving the daily barrage of verbal attacks on your character and professionalism. However, in the end, you have to be your most powerful advocate. You need to build your own armor to survive. I repeated my mantra, "I will not be broken" throughout the day, exercised my brain and body daily, and took care of me first. In the end, you learn very quickly:

"You're braver than you believe, and stronger than you seem, and smarter than you think."-Pooh.

What did I learn? The Good, the Bad, the Ugly. THE GOOD: Currently, I am the Facilitator for the Student Bullying Group on the National Education Association network. Going through this bullying ordeal has better prepared me to lead this group. It has helped me make personal connections and become an active advocate for Bully Prevention across the America. I conduct conferences and webinars on bullying, children's mental health issues, teen suicide prevention, and stress on children. I have significantly improved my mental and physical health with the gift of time. I've realized who my real friends are and have made new ones. I have restored and revitalized self-confidence and renewed respect in my abilities as a school counselor and as a person.

THE BAD: I was forced to retire – not the way I wanted to end a 32-year career. I was banned from working for my school district ever again. I've lost friendships, and I worked in a hostile workplace for the past six years.

THE UGLY: There are no winners in a bullying situation. The effects of bullying CAN and DO LAST A LIFETIME. But the one thing I had on my side was the truth and the courage to tell it.

FOUR PIECES OF ADVICE:

1. Trust yourself. Take care of 'YOU." Put your emotional and physical needs first.
2. Be Proactive- Seek professional support, help, and legal advice. Do not wait and hope it will get better.
3. Document, document, document... every meeting, email, conversation.
4. Keep your sense of humor - you will need it.

Suzie Gannett is a Facilitator for the Student Bullying Group on the NEA (National Education Association) network. The NEA is the largest labor union in the United States, with over 3 million members. She is a 32 year veteran educator, 7 years in the classroom and 25 as a counselor. But, it has been her personal workplace bullying story and her students' struggles with bullying, which have prepared her the most to lead the NEA-Student Bullying Group. Her goal is to raise awareness around mental health & bullying issues our young people face every day.

Join her group to raise awareness around mental health & bullying issues. You will find great resources, webinars, discussions, and speakers. Just go to: https:// mynea360.force.com, and click on Groups-Bully Free. It's FREE and Open To All! Contact Sue at sgannett@ comcast.net.

FOURTEEN

WORKPLACE BULLYING BEGINS IN SCHOOLS
Dr. Jennifer Fraser

My crisis began when I reported teacher bullying at a private school where I was hired to teach literature and drama. I was working under the Head of the Drama Department and he was conducting himself in ways I found to be highly inappropriate and hurtful to students. I learned I was one of a number of faculty speaking up to say there was a serious problem. I was witnessing harmful conduct firsthand, hearing from students directly as well as their distraught parents. However, the administrators treated me as if I was a problem employee. So I kept reporting, but also just put my head down. Quietly, I encouraged students and parents to write to the Director of the School about their concerns. The situation worsened until this teacher was "retired" early.

My crisis intensified right at that time as I heard from parents that their children had finally started to tell them the shocking truth about what teachers were saying to them under the auspices of "coaching" basketball. I put the reports I was hearing into the context of the Ministry of Education, the Teachers' Act, and the teacher guidebook on how to handle abuse reports, and realized that what children were reporting was emotional abuse. The police confirmed that what students were reporting showed a "definite pattern of emotional and verbal abuse." For me, this was a final straw. I could not cope with yet another report of teacher abuse at this school because this time, my own son was one of the victims. This is very important and a part of the story I wish I did not have to share. It shows for all of us employees that we might not fight back, discover our resources, learn what our rights are...until the stakes are very, very high; as high as one's own child being harmed.

At the request of a Board member, I began to reach out and find out if other families were concerned about the conduct of these teachers. The Headmaster asked me to take testimonies from students who wanted to report and I did. What I recorded and handed over to the Headmaster was material that would have a child suspended from school and an employee fired. By now, a large parent group discovered that certain Board members and school administrators were well aware of the abuse conditions under which students had been suffering, but they had not acted to protect students or inform parents.

This created a scenario whereby these same Board members and school administrators fought tooth and nail to ensure that the whole thing was thrown out as some kind of exaggeration or hyper-sensitivity or parental carry-on. They could not afford for the truth of their abject failure to protect students to come knocking at their door. Turns out they had been informed at least a year previous about the abuse. This was extremely hurtful and psychologically damaging to the students who spoke up and reported the abuse. As a teacher in the school system where I am watching conduct that is remarkably manipulative and harmful to students — including my son — I had to draw on resources to stay sane and fight back.

I went to my doctor to ask if I should take a stress leave. She looked me in the eye and said, "Will the students be compelled to attend school under these conditions?" and I replied a quiet, "Yes." She then said, "You can't have a stress leave. You need to hold your head up high, go into that place day in day out and ensure those kids are okay. You have to stand between them and what will happen." She was right. The students who spoke up — certainly some of them — were exposed by the Headmaster to one of the bullying teachers. So much for the promised confidentiality. Next thing you know, peers are bullying, teachers are acting out. The students who spoke up were under a full-on bullying regime. Previously, our son was a popular, happy kid. After the Headmaster exposed him, he became riddled with anxiety, unable to function, depressed. He did not write his exams in grade 11 or grade 12. He began to have panic attacks. The Headmaster exempted him with his new diagnosis of PTSD. However, although at least 14 kids reported four teachers as abusive, the Headmaster never stopped the teachers, nor did he publicly exonerate the kids who gave testimonies and interviews *on his request* to report on the teachers.

I had colleagues shun me, aggressively glare at me, and follow me. We had a spotlight on our house for hours. We had lug nuts taken off our car's wheels. We had to suffer day in, day out by what was being done to our son. However, we fought back and continued to fight back. Standing behind us is an amazing group of parents. We went to national media and our story was front page with a full two-page inside story in the most widely-read paper in our country. We had an investigative journalist television show cover our story. Drawing on my academic training and previous publishing, I did extensive research and wrote a book about what happened. I hoped to make social change that would help all children, not just the ones harmed in this particular situation.

Required by law, I reported to the Commissioner for Teacher Regulation in our province; however, he dismissed the students' claims and appeared to have breached many standards in his office. The file is under review with the Ombudsperson's Office in British Columbia. This file has been with them for almost three years and families feel that there is no hope. The families have encountered so much mishandling of abused children, educational regulations, private school exemptions, government failures that they, and especially their children, no longer have any belief in justice or proper treatment for students who have been brutalized by a system that claims zero tolerance for peer bullying.

Have the young people recovered from what was done? No. Psychologists, psychiatrists, and now neuroscientists tell us that bullying by peers — let alone emotional abuse by caretakers — leave scars on the brain. It doesn't heal like a bruise or even a broken bone. It leaves scars. Our son still reports nightmares, waking in sweat, insomnia, panic attacks, and performance anxiety. He is successful at university so a lawyer may simply dismiss his suffering in a court of law, but bottom line: he'll never be the same person. His days are a battle to feel good. He'll never pursue his passion again. Is it okay to take this away from a student?

I have been successful simply by fighting and living with failure. I did a huge amount of research. I wrote a book. I write daily on Twitter or Facebook about the bullying of children — not by other children — but by adults. It's taboo. It's the elephant in the room and this condoned conduct in the school system results in workplace bullying because the system engrains early on that if you bully others — you will be successful and rewarded. You will be powerful. This message is far too often branded onto children in the educational world whether in the classroom or the sports field. Some of them take this learning into the workplace. They reenact what was taught to them when they were young and impressionable. They watched a system first hand that made speaking up a risk, a big risk. They learned that keeping quiet would result in less hurt, less damage. Why would these young people not take these hard-earned lessons into the workplace? What is too often learned in classrooms and on the court or fields is that if you bully, you will have power; you will have control; no one will question you. You will be rewarded. These are lessons learned in school or home that create incredibly dysfunctional workplaces. But no one will look at the teachers of bullying. Who are they? No one will speak up and say this must stop.

How do I know? I learned first-hand. However, the school administrators, educational authorities and lawyers made a mistake in trying to silence me: I am a researcher and a writer. I care about kids. I've been a teacher for over twenty years and I am a mother. I will not keep quiet, not look away, not ignore, not pretend or act like abuse is not happening. I will not employ euphemisms like "motivating" when I see colleagues "destroying" kids. It's time for change. I tried to hold them accountable with a lawsuit, but on a teacher's salary, I could not afford "justice." They were able to access the school coffers to mount their defense so I didn't really have a chance. Plus, they had the Commissioner for Teacher Regulation condemning the children for being "too sensitive" and for *hearing* the teachers' "obscenities." When children are faulted for the abuse they report, you are fighting a losing battle.

Still, the neuroscience is chilling. Bullying — let alone emotional abuse — causes brain damage. Why laws aren't being written, educators informed, schools proactive, I don't know. I am successful; I have recovered simply because I will speak until I can no longer. I'll strive to let all know that children are vulnerable and thus we must protect them; not just their bodies, but also their brains.

My advice to those who want bullying to stop on the playground and in the workplace: look hard at those adults who teach bullying whether it's at home or at school. They once taught racism and sexism and homophobia in homes and in classrooms with impunity. They once entwined these sick lessons into sports. But it's time to reset and rethink what we do. It's time to bring in laws like England that makes emotional abuse — adults bullying children — illegal. It's criminal now in the UK to bully children and make it seem like a good strategy to excel in the workplace. If we truly want to stop workplace bullying, we need to look at its origin in the raising of children. Make those who bully children have serious consequences and the world of workplace bullying will change radically for the better.

FIVE PIECES OF ADVICE:

1. Report abuse and document everything: dates, times, places, suffering, details, and words spoken.
2. Strive to address the abuse with administrators on email or audio. Keep a record.
3. Report to government watchdogs who should protect victims.
4. Be alert to manipulations, lies, cover-ups, and gas-lighting.
5. Go to the best investigative journalists who can tell the story.

Jennifer Fraser has a PhD in Comparative Literature from University of Toronto. An avid researcher and publishing author, her third book, "Teaching Bullies: Zero Tolerance on the Court or in the Classroom," tells the full story of what happened to the students who reported being bullied by teachers. The story is set in the context of research from psychiatry, psychology and neuroscience that combines to show we really need to address the bullying crisis in our workplaces and schools.

You can connect with Jennifer at:
- *https://twitter.com/teachingbullies*
- *https://www.facebook.com/TeachingBullies/*
- *JenmFraser@Shaw.ca*

FIFTEEN

BEATING THE ODDS
Rose-Marie Vieira

M y story begins in 2008. I had just accepted a position as an Office Manager with a small mom & pop company that was run by a husband and wife. I was a bit uneasy to be working for a couple, but they seemed nice, so I accepted the job despite my unease.

After only 3 months into my employment, the husband came to me and asked that I "convince" his wife to go along with a decision he was making. I told him that I did NOT want to be in the middle of it, and that I would not agree to manipulating his wife. He got quite angry and told me that as my employer, I was to do what I was told to do. I informed him that it was against my personal as well as workplace principles. From then on, it was tough going. He would look for ways to be unhappy with my performance.

Shortly thereafter, he started hiring additional employees, with the threat that at some point, he would be hiring someone "over" me, since I didn't know how to "play ball." He kept that promise, and hired a woman that he and his wife knew through their children's school PTA. She was as difficult to be around as he was, and clearly had no problem with manipulating others.

One day, my father-in-law passed away and I was very upset at the loss. At the same time, the office was being rearranged to accommodate the recent hires. One of the things the new girl was doing was closing off access to one of the two doors to my office. I protested that it was not only a fire hazard, but that I was uncomfortable with having that door blocked. She got real ugly and snarled, "Oh go put your big girl panties on and get over yourself!" I was rather distraught that this new person could be so nasty towards me without even knowing me. I went outside the building and had myself a good cry. A total stranger from a local tour company stopped by as I was crying, to see if I was okay and in need of help. I shrugged my shoulders and asked, "Do you know of any job openings? – I work for a real a$$hat!" He said, "Sorry, no – but I hope you find something!" He gave me a hug and said be strong and that I would be ok.

During this time period, my boss was engaging in more and more bullying. He would yell at me constantly for the slightest of infractions, and call me stupid and other names. We shared office space in an old building where talking echoed within the hallways. One day, another tenant heard how my boss was treating me and actually came over to our office to "have a talk" with my boss on how badly he was treating me.

In another episode, a woman from another office on our floor came to me and said if I ever needed some private space during a difficult moment, I was free to come to her office any time. I even looked into laws that might protect me against his behavior, but was told by the Department of Labor, that although immoral, it was not illegal to mistreat employees. I was SHOCKED! I was short of money, so I wasn't able to seek any legal help for protection, nor could I afford medical attention for the daily headaches and stomach pains I was increasingly enduring.

A few months down the road, things started to really take a turn for the worse as the company expanded and we needed a larger space. I immediately recognized that I would no longer have the "safety net" of knowing that tenants were looking out for me. While they were planning how to situate each employee, they determined that my space was going to be in an oversized closet at the new location. Thankfully, they weren't that good at planning, and my desk did not fit in that space and they had to include me in the "bull pen."

As things got progressively worse, and I cried on my way into work and cried on my way home each day, I would pray for relief and a way out. I only put up with all of this all this time (1.5 years) because I own a home and feared losing it. Everything came to a head the week before

Christmas when I was bringing in a dolly with a heavy box of copy paper. Rather than ask me if he could help, he grabbed the dolly out of my hand and flung it across the room, saying, "You're in my way!" I marched into his wife's office and said, "This just CANNOT continue this way any longer, I am getting ill from how badly I am being treated!" I got fired that day. He turned to me and said, "And forget about collecting unemployment – NO ONE has ever beaten me!"

Little did he know, that once things started getting bad while I was there, I was keeping a journal of everything he did and said. When I applied for unemployment benefits, I told them about the journal as my proof of what went on there. Although they fought me THREE times against collecting unemployment, happily I WON all three times!

My advice to others is that as soon as you recognize something is not right, keep a record of EVERTYTHING – I had emails that I printed out, my journal, and even eye-witnesses. I was unable to even talk about my experience for over a year without crying. When I applied for jobs, I actually broke down and cried when asked why I left my last job.

Then I met this woman who was a victim of workplace bullying who helped me get through all the trauma. It was a form of PTSD – Post-Traumatic Stress Disorder. Her name is Dawn Westmoreland and she now travels the world sharing her story and working to stop workplace bullying. Because of this experience, I have become a much stronger person than I was AND I will NOT tolerate this kind of behavior from ANYONE – and I was tested not long after. I am also the first person to speak up if I see anyone else being targeted for bullying of any kind. I am also grateful that just recently I had the pleasure of coming across the couple that came to my defense so many times when the company was in that first building – and was able to thank them.

Currently, I am in a job where I am appreciated and treated wonderfully. I LOVE my new job! I am even bringing my current co-workers on that same local tour where the stranger had stopped to see me that day I was crying outside.

FIVE PIECES OF ADVICE:

1. Keep a journal of everything said and done that was hurtful.
2. No matter what, do your job so that the boss cannot use that against you.
3. Keep and print out any emails that show any kind of proof on your behalf. They will go through and delete those when things come to a head.
4. Surround yourself with a support system of friends and family.
5. If at all possible, seek medical help if needed. This is also documentation.

SIXTEEN

SOMETIMES OUR BEST LESSONS COME IN UGLY WRAPPING PAPER
Dawn Marie Westmoreland

I looked in the mirror at the mental-health ward, and I saw the reflection of a bully. I was looking at myself in the mirror. After two years of horrendous bullying for being a government "whistleblower," I had endured unthinkable retaliation that had nearly destroyed me. I continued looking at myself in the metal mirror, while mentally telling myself, "I hate you." I was sick of the inner bully inside of me that kept telling me I was a victim. It was time to take charge of my life and stand up to my own workplace bullying and discrimination.

As an HR expert, with over 27 years of experience and multiple degrees, I had realized that many of my former coworkers and supervisors were family and friends of management. Most of the employees were Caucasian and there were only five black employees out of 550 employees. I suspected illegal hiring and promotions within my government agency. I reported my managers to the Office of Special Counsel in Washington D.C. because nepotism is a prohibited personnel practice in all government agencies.

As soon as my managers knew of my actions, someone began tampering with my personal phone, and I was placed on administrative leave with false charges placed against me for about 100 days. I worked in a hostile environment while being denied a reasonable medical commendation as a disabled federal employee. I had served 20 years in the Air Force and became injured on active duty. My neck and back were injured. I could not work in my present job without asking for a medical accommodation, which followed the guidelines of the American Disability Act (ADA).

At this time, my job involved working on a computer most of the day. I worked on two monitors that were non-adjustable on metal pipes. My work environment was not ergonomic or safe for me. My management chose to ignore the American Disability Act (ADA) requirements I needed. I suffered in pain working in a very uncomfortable and physically challenging work environment. Fortunately, I am a strong woman of faith, but everyone has a breaking point. Every Sunday evening was a painful experience for me. I knew I had to go back to a hostile work environment on Monday. It was very depressing at the time. I was also going through a divorce and trying to pay off bills too.

Hateful looks and stalking are very common when you are experiencing bullying. Since I reported about 15 federal supervisors and managers for prohibited personnel practices, I became a target for unmerciful retaliation. For example, I was "passed over" for numerous promotions, falsely charged with absences without leave, and my supervisors invaded my medical privacy records over and over again. It's also very unnerving when someone tells you to be careful of leaving food or drinks in the refrigerator. I was not allowed to work from my home on my computer like another disabled federal employee I knew who worked in the same job. It's hard to believe that people can act this way. While even bullies can become victims, you must nevertheless hold them accountable if they are bullying others.

Looking back, I have had people ask me why I did not walk away from this job. There was a part of me that knew I was going through all this awful experience for a reason. I kept great documentation of everything that was going on at work. I researched employment laws and federal regulations that applied to my situation.

I compiled many pages of employment laws and documentation. I then filed charges with the Equal Employment Opportunity Commission (EEOC) because I was being discriminated for my disabilities when my managers tried to fire me and refused to accommodate my disabilities per the protocol of the ADA. After my managers began to bully and harass me, I filed retaliation charges because it's illegal for anyone in your workplace to harass you for filing an EEOC discrimination case.

The long-term stress landed me in the mental health ward for a few days. I was on antidepressants and anti-anxiety medications at this time. I admit that I was so obsessed with holding my bullies accountable that I was not practicing self-care and finding balance in my life. I spent many hours working on my cases, but neglected my well-being. The third day in the mental health ward, I was allowed to take a shower, and as I was looking at myself in the metal mirror, I decided the biggest bully in my life was myself for thinking I was a "victim." It was an awful time in my life, but I decided I would no longer allow myself to feel like I did not have control over my own happiness and personal power. I still had to wait for about a year for my EEOC hearing.

That year was very tough for me. I was super broken in spirit at times and also in the pocket book! What's alarming is that most people have to wait four or five years to get a hearing with the EEOC. There were 19 severe charges of retaliation that bumped my cases up to a speedier hearing. I realized I was punished for speaking out against alleged prohibited personnel practices of my former managers. My pay was cut off permanently, and my financial portrait was severely compromised. It was sad to watch my credit scores go from "outstanding" to "poor" in a matter of a few months. That was one of the hardest things for me to accept. However, I learned to live within a very tight budget, and I learned to meditate so I could learn to quiet the chaos in my life. Well, sometimes our "gifts" in our life come in "ugly wrapping paper."

I had to experience being severely bullied and working through it all to become the person I am today. I must admit that I was very proud of myself for compiling and submitting all the required documentation that would later land me a "settlement" with my former federal agency. It's interesting that so many employees out there think they must have a witness to have credible proof of workplace bullying or discrimination. This simply is not true! If you know what you are doing and have the courage to stand up for your rights, you can move mountains! However, practice self-care as it's easy for stress to harm your well-being.

It was really hard to sell my large beautiful home and move into a smaller older rental home, but I have learned - it's not the end of the world! Selling some of my nicer furniture and home items kept my head above water. I was always telling myself, "This is only temporary."

I have a great ending, despite all of it. I ended up settling with this government agency and without a "gag order" to be silent, so that I could share my story and help others who are experiencing workplace bullying and discrimination. Today, I am a HR consultant, speaker, author, and coach.

My mission is to empower others so that they can also stand up to workplace bullying and discrimination.

I have helped many private sector and federal employees by sharing my story and my expertise. Attorneys are now hiring me to learn how to support their clients when they are facing retaliation and experiencing discrimination. They are always amazed that I refused to sign a settlement "gag order" that would keep me from sharing my experience. You can do that when you have courage, HR knowledge, and tenacity to hold your bullies accountable.

I will share an important tip about sharing your bullying story on social media. It feels great to share your concerns or your victories on social media. It can feel gratifying to get approval or "likes" on your posts. But—can your social media posts backfire on you? Yes, they can. If you are venting about your workplace bullying and using a person's name, you could be committing defamation of character. So be careful what you say online.

It is very cathartic to share how you feel about your workplace bullying situation, but do it with people you trust. Pay attention to the people you surround yourself with because their "energy" will rub off on you. Reach out to support groups or create your own, so you can get the help you need and the support you deserve. Be smart and remember, "You are always on Parade." You are observed by people who are visible and invisible in your life.

You can find helpful resources to stand up to workplace bullying and discrimination at my website: www.WorkplaceBullyingSupport.com

FIVE MORE PIECES OF ADVICE:

1. Document your bullying experience and hand-carry it home.
2. Find a mentor, attorney or HR consultant to support you.
3. Keep balance and peace in your life.
4. Set healthy boundaries with everyone in your life.
5. Don't ever let the worst bully be yourself.

Dawn Marie Westmoreland is the founder of Dawn Westmoreland Consulting LLC. She was sent to Washington D.C in April 2015 to educate Senators on the need to protect Government Whistleblowers and to hold government employees accountable for illegal activities. Since 2014, Dawn has helped numerous employees to standup to workplace bullying and discrimination through her radio interviews, magazine articles, and presentations she gives across the United States. She has been lauded by the Christian Science Monitor for empowering employees through her work. Dawn is the author of "The Empowered Whistleblower" A Practical and Spiritual Path to Personal Power. Her second book, "Solutions to Workplace Bullying and

Discrimination" will be on the market soon, which provides comprehensive guidance to employees. Dawn's current clients include government leaders, political teams, government agencies, private companies, attorneys, mental health professionals, spiritual leaders, and employees.

You can connect with Dawn at:
- *ConsultWithDawn@gmail.com*
- *www.WorkplaceBullyingSupport.com*
- *https://www.linkedin.com/in/ dawnmariewestmoreland/*
- *https://www.facebook.com/ WorkplaceBullyingandDiscriminationSupport/*
- *https://twitter.com/DawnRespect*

SEVENTEEN

ACCOUNTABILITY STARTS
AT THE TOP
Rachelle Le Blanc

M y bullying experience didn't start with me. This employee and I are on the organizational chart at the same level. Within the first six months of his employment, I, as the Human Resource personnel, received a large overwhelming amount of complaints about him. They ranged from sexual harassment, gender discrimination, insensitive comments regarding weight and personal appearance. In meetings, he would have a hit list and call out names of people that owed him things. He crossed and jump roped over bullying and straight up illegal harassment consistently.

Watching my coworkers being treated this way was weighing on me physically and morally. I didn't see him held accountable once. The comments weren't made to me but I was sometimes in the same room and hearing them is just as bad as receiving them. Most of the time the reports came from witnesses and not victims.

The company culture history was often used as an excuse for his behavior. He was used to managing the business he owned. Now that he was an employee, he couldn't separate from owner to employee. He would disrespect, harass and offend employees when he didn't get his way so they would respond by shutting down and avoiding him. He justified his actions of making comments such as, "If a man was in your position it would get done," and, "That workplace accident happened on Valentine's Day so it is a hickey and not a rash; you should look into that." He would say he was the one being bullied because he couldn't get the other employees to work with him and they were withholding information from him.

I finally raised my hand after a year. The reason I hadn't said anything previously was because I had seen other people complain about him and nothing changed. I didn't want to be labeled as weak, trouble or someone who complains a lot. I was under the impression that he has a personal relationship with someone in the Executive Management Team and I didn't want to be retaliated against. The following incidents were my deal breakers:

1. Every time I put out a memo, email, or policy change, I would get a copy of it in my mail box the next day covered in red ink noting all mistakes. I

told him directly that it bothers me and his response was that he does it on his own time and that he is going to keep doing it. When I approached my manager, he told me it was not appropriate. When he was spoken to about it, he said that he wasn't going to stop.

2. I got an email from the bully highlighting his concerns for females working after hours and how unsafe it was and that it was "more of a guy's job." I have never been a feminist but I did take a women's studies class in college and I am a fan of Sheryl Sandberg and the Lean In movement. My mother is a CFO and I have always been scared of her. She told me she would never ask for a raise, and that if she deserves one she knows her boss will offer it to her. My conclusion from everything I have learned is that in order to be successful I need to raise my hand, which I have never had trouble doing. My foundation and values come from my family. In my family chores were never broken up female and male. We organized on each other's strengths as a team. It never crossed my mind that the gender gap was a real thing until this happened. The bully made me feel very conflicted.

I was embarrassed of being a woman and I wanted to apologize for it.

I felt angry. I was never told that I was different because of gender. I didn't believe that people actually felt this way. I was a millennial caught in the headlights.

3. I was on a conference call and the bully came in and put a magazine article on my desk with the headline: "This Time, its HR getting Fired." The article was four months old. I was concerned that he sat on it for that long and still thought it was appropriate. If you were to read the article, it is about a startup benefits company and had used the headline to get attention. When he was spoken to about it, I was told that he hadn't actually read the article and that I was too sensitive.

I felt hopeless in this situation. When I got the nerve to raise my hand I was successful for the first time. He refused to acknowledge my pain, threw it in my face and walked out after screaming at my boss. I have never seen someone act out violently, especially to their boss and still be employed. He looked untouchable.

From there he had double the amount of complaints over the next year against him. I could feel in the culture how much it was affecting me as well as the other employees. The complaints were serious and we could get in big legal trouble. They ranged again from aggressive behavior, aggressive tones, threatening employees, violating HIPPA laws, sexual conduct and gender discrimination. He told other employees that they are not allowed to go to Human Resources (that's me) and they could only go to him.

The final incident with him brought me to an all-time low. I left like I had gotten sucker punched and I was physically sick to my stomach. An employee came to me and apologized for making a complaint but she felt very uncomfortable. She said that she knew the bully was allowed to act this way but she could no longer work with him. She said the bully had made previous comments about how small she was physically and she had always brushed it off. But this time he was helping her carry something, and she told him to be careful, and his response was that if it spilled, she would have to lick it off him.

Being in Human Resources is different than being a normal employee; especially, if you work in a small company. You don't have a strong support system and you can't be emotional. Outside of work I do have a great support system but saying too much is not appropriate or professional. When I speak to my parents and get their insight, they usually don't have much to say. My Dad is a CEO and somehow doesn't understand what Human Resources is and my mom's response is that, "You can only do the best you can do," and my favorite, "Kill them with kindness!" When you work in Human Resources it is not hard to be caught in the cross fire and not be seen as an employee. My job is to advise my Executive Team and let them make the hard decisions.

If you don't believe in the company culture, values and management team, then you need to find a workplace that does. In your personal life, you wouldn't marry someone or have a good friend that doesn't have your same values, and work shouldn't be different.

I have learned the following important things throughout this experience:

1. A person's perception is reality. An organization that is adaptable to change and conflict has clear communication and expectations. Tough conversations are awkward, uncomfortable and people avoid them. They are also time sensitive and you only get one chance. If you don't act quickly you're going to end up with a culture of fear.

2. You do not want all of your hard work and success to be overshadowed by one bad decision. Once you change people's minds or lose their trust, it is impossible to rebuild. That one moment of weakness is not worth it.

3. You can't change people. This employee was lost and damaged way beyond what I could provide for him. Opinions that were developed early in someone's life are strong.

The employee eventually exited the company and people still talk about it. When his exit was announced, the room was silent and there was no cheering. Employees were happy that it was over but they were sad that he couldn't understand. Because of his behavior, I think exiting was the proper decision, but I do think he should have exited much sooner. If anti-bullying was open and known, we would be better to hold people accountable and the employees who like that kind of work environment will exit themselves out.

Accountability starts with executive leadership and they should be held accountable by the entire company. Everyone needs to communicate to those who aren't abiding to company culture. Give people a chance to decide if your company is right for them so you don't have to make the decision for them.

FIVE PIECES OF ADVICE:

1. Take a stance as a group. Tell your coworkers what you expect from them and what they can expect from you.
2. Ask your coworkers how they want to be treated.
3. Ask your coworkers how they want to be communicated with.
4. Frequently run through your code of ethics with your employees and ask them to give examples of violations or successful stories.
5. Act fast and communicate the outcome.

EIGHTEEN

YOU ARE STRONGER THAN YOU THINK
Laura

In 2015, I left my job of 14 years to seek something better; however, it was a total nightmare. Unfortunately, I had a bully supervisor and was required to pass a 1-year probation. Within 2 months, in a closed-door meeting, I was told what not to do; no talking to my co-workers; not entitled to a break; no leaving my office without prior notification (except to the restroom or lunch), etc. I felt like I was a child asking for permission. These may seem like normal things a boss tells an employee, but when you are the only one being reprimanded for these things then you start to feel singled out.

It is then that I decided to choose my battles. If it was work related, I would give her the benefit of the doubt. But if it wasn't work related, then it was personal. And that's when I would defend myself. Needless to say, things did become personal and we had many more closed-door meetings. It wasn't until 9 months of trying to defend myself, that I related everything to her boss (Director). He listened to me, but ultimately dismissed everything with "that is how she is" and "things will get better." Next, I met with his boss (VP) who also listened and I felt I could trust her except she handed me off to Employee Relations.

By now, my boss wanted to extend my probation by 6 months without speaking to the Director, the VP, or me first. Next, I met with a representative from Employee Relations where I inquired about filing a grievance and he told me that only regular, non-probationary employees could file a grievance. Since I was still on probation, I was not allowed to file a formal grievance. In a 2-hour mediation meeting, the outcome from Employee Relations was summed up as "listen to your boss and do what she tells you." The worst part from all these meetings was that bullying was the norm and I was treated like a trouble maker that ultimately earned an unsatisfactory evaluation. This was the first time I had received an unsatisfactory evaluation.

After almost a year of turmoil and speaking with family, friends, and co-workers, I decided to seek counseling from our EAP (Employee Assistance Program). At the first session, I told him that after speaking to the leadership team and asking for help, no one truly listened or cared about my situation. I came to believe that I was making a big deal about it. I questioned my self-worth and competence to do my job. I couldn't believe that I, an employee with several degrees and almost 20 years working at the same company, but in different departments, could allow someone to control my well-being. It was overwhelming to realize that one person can make you feel paranoid and self-conscious while causing stress, high blood-pressure, nausea, and depression. I was very vulnerable because I was on probation and could lose my job and all the while I was being made to feel inferior.

The EAP gave me two pieces of documentation: 1. Our policy on bullying and 2. Information from the Workplace Bullying website (http://www.workplacebullying.org/individuals/problem/being-bullied/). Our policy had been there for several years; however, no one in the leadership team mentioned it, let alone appeared to follow and enforce it. The workplace bullying information helped tremendously because it validated my situation to be real and not imaginary. I didn't realize that I was being bullied. It is something you don't think will happen to you, especially at work where we are all adults and professionals. Once I was able to put a name to my situation, the outlook for my future became clearer. It took only 2 sessions with the EAP to not feel so alone and know that someone truly cared. I literally began putting myself back together.

I couldn't have survived being bullied at work if it wasn't for the support and love from God, my family, and close friends. One way that helped me heal was by talking about the incident to anyone that would listen in comparison to the leadership team. I made sure to document everything that happened with dates, conversations, and who was involved in case I did file a grievance. I have always had a strong relationship with God and believe whole heartedly in the power of prayer. Family and friends prayed for me. I prayed for me, and believe it or not, I prayed for my boss. It was then that I decided to let God carry my cross and lift up my burdens. I began feeling at ease, then at peace. I believe this happened because she no longer had control of me. I no longer allowed her to have control of me!

I was already knee-deep in the healing stage when I was transferred to another department due to budget cuts. I have since then forgiven my boss and time and prayer will help me get to the "forgive and forget" stage. My best piece of advice to you is this: Do not try to tackle a bullying situation alone because that's what it feeds on. Seek help immediately from family, friends, or supportive professionals.

THREE PIECES OF ADVICE:

1. Faith - Have faith in God to help you through this! Have faith in yourself. You are stronger than you think!
2. Forgive - Forgive the people that hurt you with their actions, words, or indifference.

Forgive yourself! After all, you did not ask to be bullied.

3. Family, Friends, & Professionals – Choose wisely. Only a select group of family, friends, and professionals will be genuinely concerned with your well-being.

You can connect with Laura at:

- *Marikoki777@gmail.com*
- *http://www.workplacebullying.org/individuals/problem/being-bullied/*

NINETEEN

REALIZING YOUR POWER: NAVIGATING YOUR WAY BACK TO TRANQUILITY

Anonymous

This is a story about why I love my college's mission, but am ashamed of its culture. I have been bullied for the past three years. I had a distinguished career prior to being hired as an Assistant Professor at a college. I am a lesbian, woman of color with a PhD. I am the only person of color in my academic department. My boss, who was the department head at the college where I taught, targeted me relentlessly. My friends and family say I was targeted because I was younger, more talented, and more popular amongst our students. Not only did my boss target me, but he created an environment in the workplace where others had permission by example to bully me.

I was particularly surprised when a female professor also started to bully me. I initially thought how could another female take part in such destructive behavior? Wouldn't she want to see a junior faculty member succeed? I was mobbed by coworkers. My reputation was damaged by my boss and coworkers spreading rumors about me and repeatedly undermining my contributions. He continuously set me up to fail by not providing clear expectations; I was removed from key positions and responsibilities and discouraged from participating in higher profile working groups. My evaluation was lowered and the language was deliberately weakened. When I asked my boss to explain or at least provide me with feedback that I can improve on for the next year, he never even responded to any of my emails.

My identity as an intelligent, black, lesbian woman was never respected. My unique perspectives about the world were never valued. Ironically, my college, on paper, boasts about diversity and inclusion as essential ingredients to achieving our mission of graduating men and women who can tackle 21st Century global issues. My college nominated me for an award to "celebrate" the diversity we have on our campus, yet I have never felt welcomed or included. It's tokenism. It's shameful. It's morally despicable. The institution claims credit for having someone like me on its faculty, while creating an environment not fit for any human to endure. Bullying is "status-blind" harassment and the targets are usually different in some way.

My college does not have a bullying policy. It has a general conduct policy and an anti-harassment/discrimination policy for protected classes. Initially when the bullying first occurred, I mustered up the courage to confront my boss directly. I had many bad bosses in the past and thought the best course of action was to be direct and talk through it like adults. Then he blamed workplace tensions on my same-sex marriage and conveyed if I complained again he would give me a bad evaluation. I knew in his response this was new territory for me and this was not your typical "bad boss" situation. From there I decided it was appropriate to have conversations with his direct boss. I was told that he was a good performer and that we just needed to keep working on the relationship. I contacted HR professionals for guidance. They told me that maybe the problem was me because I was the only one raising concerns. Over the next year, I then contacted the Civil Rights professionals, and they told me they would investigate my allegations. The investigator selected was friends with my boss. This investigator told me inappropriate things about his wife and how she resolves conflict during his interview of me. He concluded that my allegations were not substantiated.

Now it was no secret that I was utilizing resources to end the bullying. My boss retaliated. His looks, stares, non-verbals in meetings all escalated. My boss sent out an email to my department which detailed the obituary of an employee who complained about unethical behavior to upper management but was ignored. When I notified HR and counselors of this intimidating behavior, I was told the only option was to file another grievance. So I did.

As if the first time wasn't humiliating enough, the second time around the assigned investigator was also friends with my boss. They were seen laughing and joking in the hallway before interviews of employees. All employees in my department were interviewed; however, my boss demanded that we tell him when our meetings were scheduled with the investigator. This definitely did not seem impartial or treating my allegations with dignity. I departed my office to head towards my interview but shrinked back in the opposite direction because I saw my boss lurking outside the door to the interview room. My heart was pounding and it felt like I couldn't breathe. I eventually made it to the interview room only to realize that the investigator had interviewed everybody else and it was apparent his mind was already made up.

The investigator in his final report stated that it was my boss's department and that the environment was fine. The institution then sent an email to my entire department stating that there was a personality conflict between two people. One email dismissed the reality that I was targeted. One email further created an environment where my peers could continue to blame me for "stirring something up." As the investigator stated, the environment was fine except for me complaining about it. This was a very dark day. I questioned everything about my college, its values, and the people around me who witnessed me being bullied but did not speak up.

From the beginning, I always had a strong support network of allies in other departments, and supportive family, friends, physicians and counselors. However, over the 3 years, my health had significantly declined. My emotional, spiritual, and physical energy were practically depleted. I developed gastrointestinal issues, anxiety, depression, and suicidal thoughts. I knew I had to make a decision about my future. I knew that this was not fair to my wife. I knew that I loved teaching. So I reflected deeply and decided to change my entire outlook on the situation. I am an introvert by nature. Growing up in social circles where I was usually the "only one," I realized I had a lifetime of understanding human conditions such as insecurity and fear. I had a lifetime of experiences where I persevered because I stayed true to my authentic self and values. I have learned in my life that things are not fair or rational, but things can be understood. I knew I was experiencing pain and suffering in the arc between expectations and reality. I knew how incredibly unfair and hurtful it was for my college to exploit me externally, and marginalize me internally. I knew how irrational it was for my college to boast about the strengths of diversity and inclusion and yet obstruct my ability to perform and educate young adults.

My decision was simple but the most difficult decision I ever made. I decided to stay for my students. I knew that if I was being bullied and had no avenues for recourse, then what options existed for my students? I knew that we had an institutional problem with bullying that did not end with faculty. Students confided in me about their experiences and I was one of very few faculty members where they could have that safe conversation. I spoke about this decision extensively with my physicians, counselors, and most importantly, my wife. They were all supportive of me standing my ground because they realized it was my calling to serve those who do not have a voice. I am not a martyr. I just love my students and want to be the best role model for them so they can be successful in society. As an educator, that is my calling. And in today's society of increasing incivility, I wanted to be a part of the solution. I wanted to demonstrate to them how to mentor and advocate for others who also do not have a voice and are being marginalized or bullied.

Looking back, I would have complained louder, earlier, and even more directly. Standing up for myself improved my health and self-esteem overall. I was in control of how and when I complained. I would have been more aggressive about finding people who understand bullying who are also in management positions to take action. Bullies don't stop unless they are told to stop. My decision to leave will also be simple but difficult. I'll leave when I wake up one morning and realize I've had enough. I will be more enriched knowing I did everything I could to improve the lives of others. My wife will help me with that assessment and I value her judgment. My health or sanity is not worth being the target of bullying. I have helped my institution understand bullying more (more than they even know) and I know my efforts matter to my students and other faculty who are bullied. Knowing when to stay and knowing when to leave is a true test of personal values, resilience, and leadership.

FIVE PIECES OF ADVICE

1. If you are deciding to stay, find an advocate in a position of power over the bully who will take action.
2. Document everything.
3. If you are deciding to leave, leave early and with your dignity.
4. Don't question your instincts.
5. Continue to love yourself, be kind to yourself, and never blame yourself.

TWENTY

How To Manage Your Brand During a "Hot Ass Mess" Crisis!

Gwendolen Wilder, Author, Business Strategist & Motivational Consultant

M y name is Gwendolen and my experience was a bit unique because I perceived myself as a hypocrite. I owned a successful business processing complaints of discrimination, sexual harassment and workplace harassment. In my own business, I created a workplace policy which covered anti-discrimination which included bullying. If one of my contractors had an issue, it would've been resolved internally or via the EEOC.

So, why did I perceive myself as a hypocrite? I was bullied and harassed pretty much daily during my commute, in two office settings and I did nothing. My bully worked under me and was my then common law husband. I never had a reprieve. His constant psychological harassment escalated into physical domestic violence; he tried to choke me. You can discover more on how I survived inside my novel, *It's OK to Tell My Story! Surviving Common Law Domestic Violence.* I recall so many instances of workplace bullying but, one really stood out. I held weekly department manager meetings in my downtown office. During the meetings, I expected individuals to be prepared, professional, respectful and give undivided attention to the speaker. My bully never played by the rules. In meetings, he consistently spoke over me, interrupted me, tried to lead the meeting, etc.

That morning, he imparted his psychological and physical abuse onto me. Why? Because he didn't want to attend the meeting. He had been up late the night prior partying, smoking weed and was tired. Once we arrived at work, he decided he was going to stay downstairs smoking. As he began gathering his cigarettes, I headed to the elevator and said, "OK, I'll see you up there." He disgustedly replied with a smirk, "Maybe." I asked in clarification, "Excuse me?" He distastefully replied, "Just go upstairs; I'll be up there when I get there." Everyone was in place and ready to begin, except him. I played it off, extended small talk and went for coffee. When I returned, he was sitting in my seat, at the head of the table. I stated, "Ok great, now that everyone's here we can get started." As I placed my arm on my chair, as a non-verbal indicator to nudge him to move; he just sat there. I politely asked, "Do you mind, so we can get going?" He replied, "Go ahead and sit down then so we can get this started; you're already late." I was mortified, beyond embarrassed, humiliated and felt a loss of dignity.

I tried my best to not lead on to what was occurring, but the staff felt the tension. As their leader, the last thing I wanted to do was show a sign of weakness as a lady entrepreneur, owner, etc. The constant bullying made me feel defeated and a failure to myself, my team and my mission. I tried to keep my composure, started the meeting and reminded all to silence their cell phones. The entire time, he simply typed on either his cell or laptop. As I glared at him, he eventually commented, "What, go on then." To avoid further embarrassment, I hosted the meeting by walking around the room and used the white board. After the meeting ended, people couldn't leave fast enough. And there he was laughing, joking and preparing to leave. I asked, "Do you mind hanging back a minute so we could discuss something?" He replied with a smirk grin, "No, I'm going for a smoke and I'll be downstairs when you're ready." Naturally, he insisted on driving and I swear it seemed he took the extra-long route home. The entire ride and after arriving home, he laid into me like a child that stole candy from a store. I felt about two inches tall, beat down and worthless. I tried my best talking with him. But, all he responded with in between berating me was, "Don't use that EO Psychological Bullshit on me" or "For someone so smart, you are really dumb." I started second guessing myself, questioned if he was correct and if I really knew what I was doing in my job.

The effects of constant bullying, harassment and domestic violence took a toll on my life. I experienced migraines, stress, anxiety, depression, fatigue, sleeplessness, physical bruises and was hospitalized with related illnesses. I was already dealing with Post-Traumatic Stress Disorder and his actions really sent me over the top. The bullying affected my overall business. I extended hours to work in my physical office to escape him. Even though I had semi-peace, the extended hours costed my business additional expenses in office leasing, parking and support staff fees. His embarrassing actions costed me clients and my business reputation. I knew something had to change. I fell back to my cornerstone, God. I feel God aligns us with a specific set of skills which enables us to complete our purpose. My gift, other than the gift of gab, is being able to connect with people, analyze root causes and identify solutions. Thus, I analyzed myself. The first part was easy, I knew I had a bully. Next, I cataloged all bullying incidents. For each one, I identified what he said, what I perceived and facts. Then, I considered coworker interactions, liability, etc. This resulted in me revising the workplace policy with explicit language regarding bullying.

Furthermore, I reassessed his presence in meetings. I advised all managers, if they couldn't attend in person, then attend virtually and provide a written status report. Revising this procedure saved my business money and time while increasing productivity. In the USAF, I learned the importance of accountability and documentation. I decided to hold myself accountable by implementing a risk assessment. I had to remember, it wasn't just about me; it was about my staff which endured the behaviors. I kept records, used conflict management, email blasts for mandatory training, etc. This proved worthwhile. But, his increased workplace violence, domestic violence and missed deadlines caused my business thousands of dollars and credibility. His actions finally equipped me with justification to terminate him. I won the battle, but not the war. He was out of my physical workplace, but still in my home office. In retaliation, he was worse than ever. He began intruding my office space, yelling at me, interrupting calls, playing loud music, etc. Being prior military with base access, I secretly planned to seek spiritual counseling. I knew he hated grocery shopping and didn't have base access; the grocery was a perfect cover story. I met with a chaplain, bore my soul and cried for an hour. The chaplain in no uncertain terms indicated, "You need to leave or it may end badly." He also stated, "He may feel envious or jealous of your accomplishments." His words reminded me of the day I received my B.S. in Psychology. My abuser said, "It's just a piece of paper; it really doesn't mean anything." I was crushed. The chaplain's final advice: pray, trust in God and leave. Where am I now? Living my passion and loving life! As I hinted earlier, my domestic violence extended years, but I finally had the courage to leave. After I realized my "Success Begins with ME," my life has been phenomenal. My mission is bridging the gap between individual self-awareness, businesses and domestic violence using awareness, prevention and intervention. I also released my first book in 2017, working on my second, received numerous honors, etc. The best part, I gained sponsors which contributed $20K to help abuse victims.

I hate what happened, but I'm glad it did. I wouldn't change a thing because my lesson would not be the same. I learned so much about myself and used that information to encourage victims to understand, "Success Begins with Knowing It's OK to Tell the Story!" Whether the story be workplace bullying, domestic violence, sexual assault, etc. I believe God created me to be a sophisticated thinker and has placed me in a position of influence to bring awareness to all forms of workplace violence. Even more awesome, God made you an influencer as well. I encourage you to tap into your sphere of influence. Consider how you use your influence to help victims. In my upcoming book, I share 7 concepts to manage a domestic violence crisis in the workplace. The foundation consists of three tiers. First, recognize your place of influence. Intervene, share awareness or provide clarification. Talk about bullying instead of joking about it.

Comprehend certain behaviors equal bullying. Seek to understand current workplace policy, processes, referral agents, resources, etc. Second, stay in your lane. If you're not capable mentally/emotionally to assist someone - don't. The best way to assist is by engaging a referral source, i.e., HR. Third, know when it's Time to Speak Up. Step out in courage by supporting workplace policies, helping victims, speaking to bullies and inviting others to have those difficult conversations.

FOUR PIECES OF ADVICE

1. Recognize your place of Influence.
2. Stay in your lane.
3. Know when it is time to speak up.
4. Understand, "Success Begins with Knowing It's OK to Tell Your Story."

Gwendolen is an author, certified business strategist and motivational consultant (www. gwendolenwilderauthor.com). She bridges the gap in domestic violence awareness between individuals and businesses using self-awareness, business acumen and domestic violence management. Her clients include the United States Air Force and Army Installation Family Advocacy Programs, Small Business Administrations, Female Veteran Business Centers, Family Violence Prevention Services; and other nonprofits, churches and small businesses in a huge array of industries. She has made many television, newspaper and radio appearances, authored books and numerous articles, and has spoken on the topic internationally in online training and conferences. She authored, "It's OK To Tell My Story, Surviving Common Law Domestic Violence," is currently writing, "Managing Domestic Violence in the Workplace, 7 Concepts to Easily Manage Your Brand During a Crisis," created the Living, Laughing and Loving Gratitude Journal, The Wilder Success Newsletter and Turn Out the Lights Kickass Guide on Gas Lighting; just to name a few works. As testimonials, Jerome Ellis, Seymour Johnson AFB, Family Advocacy Manager quoted, "This book is revolutionary, a game changer that is altering lives of domestic violence victims in the AF one day at a time..." Erick Anderson, EEO Counselor, Captain (Ret) USAF stated, "Gwendolen's ability to apply her mastery of effective listening during client engagement ensures she fully understands their needs, desires & ambitions...she accomplishes this in a way rarely encountered in business today." Laura Ann Campbell, Founder of Truth Evolution, LLC stated "Gwendolen is nothing short of amazing, inspiring & a catalyst for positive change. She has an infectious love for life, is an aggressive supporter & champion of those unable to advocate for themselves." An Amazon reader quoted, "Having a friend in an abusive relationship, I often wondered "WHY?" Why does she stay? Why won't she leave? This book answered those questions for me. I never looked at it the way that things were presented in this book. It was an eye-opener...to the author, thank *you. Thank you for giving me a way to look at domestic abuse in another way..."*

She was fortunate enough to connect with the National Workplace Bullying Coalition to continue to share her passion and inspire others.

You can connect with Gwendolen at:
- *info@gwendolenwilderauthor.com*
- *http://gwendolenwilderauthor.com*
- *https://gwendolen-wilder.mykajabi.com*
- *https://twitter.com/infogwendolen*
- *https://www.instagram.com/gwendolenwilder/*
- *https://www.linkedin.com/in/gwendolen-wilder-b2978912a*
- *https://www.facebook.com/gwendolenwilderauthor/*
- *https://vimeo.com/204031680*

TWENTY-ONE

THE THREATENING BOSS & A HIGHLY SENSITIVE PERSON
Alan Eisenberg

I sat there across my boss's boss again. I was a 25-year-old young man working at one of the top entertainment companies in the country. It should have been a dream job for someone like me, but instead it was my lesson in having one of the worst bullying bosses in the workplace. This woman, a vice-president in the company, was yelling at me for the hundredth time, again telling me that if I couldn't prove whatever she was accusing me of this time, I was fired. It was always a threat of some sort. Of course, I was not alone. This woman put someone in tears each day. The truth is that I could hardly hear what she was saying, as my anxiety and panic attacks were in full force as she attacked me. These feelings were so familiar to me, because bullying didn't start at work. Oh no, it was a much bigger story than that.

My workplace bullying started long ago, when I was a young man between the ages of 6-13. I was relentlessly bullied during this time and learned much later that it would continue to affect me as a condition now known as complex Post-Traumatic Stress Disorder (C-PTSD). Of course, as a young boy, I had no idea of the long-term effects of bullying that are now studied and verified by professionals. But I always knew, as I got older, that I was different. What was I bullied for? I found that I am a HSP (Highly Sensitive Person) in touch with my emotions and easily affected by the emotions of others. These are not concepts that children think about while being bullied. Most ask me, "What's wrong with you?" when the question they should be asking is, "What's wrong with them?" But we are not yet wise enough to know. The problem is that once the damage was done in my youth, I spent the next 30 years dealing with low self-esteem, anxiety, anger, stress, and all the other magical things that a youth who is not helped after bullying deals with.

You probably know me, because as an adult, I was one of the many of us who struggled to let go of the past and move forward in the direction of life that we want to go. Met any bitter adults in life? Ever wonder what made them that way? But this is my story about workplace bullying. I think it is important that I share my back story so you know one of the reasons I was an easy target for further bullying at the hands of one of my bosses.

Back to my situation at this job. My familiar panic was starting to make my ears ring as she yelled. By this point, I wished she would just fire me. But that wasn't her game. It was just to see if I would cry. At least that's the way it seemed to me. It really wasn't any different than the taunting I dealt with on the playground at school.

This woman would do more than just yell at me. Many times, she would call me into her office, only to be on the phone with someone for thirty minutes to an hour as I sat there. She also would not come into work until 11 am, while the rest of us showed up early. However, she expected us all to stay until she left, which was sometimes 9 or 10 pm.

I recall one time when an overnight delivery I was to send for a television show airing didn't arrive or so she thought. By this time, I was so worried about being yelled at that I tuned into the station that Saturday and there I saw that the show wasn't on. I didn't sleep at all that weekend. I knew arriving at work that Monday there would be a note to see her immediately. I knew I overnighted the tape for the show, but she made me doubt myself. She called me in and in the predictable way, told me I would be fired if I didn't prove I had sent it. I was in a full-blown panic attack and ran to the restroom to throw up. Then I went to the computer and found the signature of the person who received the tape. I called them and they had never given it to the producer. I went to explain to her what happened. She said she didn't care and that I was to call them every time I sent a tape to make sure they got it. She still said it was my fault, but that she wasn't firing me...this time.

That was the final straw for me. Something in me broke that day. Maybe it was the fact that I knew in my heart of hearts that I didn't do anything wrong. Maybe it was just that I hadn't imagined a work life like this. Maybe it was the birth of my first son and the realization that if this continued, I wouldn't see him grow up. I thought of something that day. It was a thought about my life. I realized that I had choices in my life and for some reason, I thought about it around my death. It wasn't really morbid to me. I thought if given the choice, do I want people whose lives I affected at my funeral or a bunch of flowers sent by a company I worked for that would be putting an ad in the paper for my job at the same time? I decided there and then that I didn't want to be that workaholic who had nothing else.

Something else bothered me. Some of my co-workers actually liked this woman who abused them. To me, it was like they were enabling her. I just couldn't take it anymore. The Human Resources division of the company failed the employees as well. I would have gone to HR about it, but I first gave that advice to a co-worker. She met with HR about this issue; however, they were ineffective due to the top levels of the company. This co-worker eventually left due to the bullying. At that point I certainly had no faith in the HR department at this company. So, I got another job and left. As I look back, this job and the next few years made me realize a few things that I take with me to work today.

Work/ life balance is a necessity at work – I have to be able to work reasonable hours and be there for my family and myself. Vacation is decompression and I do not do any work during vacation. Find a stress outlet – you will have stress in your life and there needs to be an outlet. Don't bottle it in. Good ways to release stress are exercise, meditation, walks in nature or doing an activity that you are passionate about. Nobody's perfect so give up perfection – if your workplace expects you to be perfect, you will fail. No one is perfect. As humans, particularly ones new to the workforce, we will make mistakes. Work to live with mindfulness (in the now) and let it roll off. Realize that you deserve to be treated well. Try to remember the "what's wrong with them" lesson and give up self-blame when someone else bullies you.

As for me, I got a new job and never looked back. Well, that's not really true, I did keep up with what happened to my workplace bully. A few years after I moved on, she was fired. Last I heard, she was selling handbags. I do believe in karma. I also decided to write my own bullying stories and now have authored two books and run a company called Bullying Recovery. Yes, it is so important that we know we are not alone and that many of us exist who have been bullied, whether at school or work. It's not right anywhere and it is my dream now to help people recover and move on from the damage bullying causes. Every day I feel great about doing that work and that makes a world of difference.

FIVE PIECES OF ADVICE:

1. Find a trusted professional, friend or family member to talk to about your situation.
2. Take out your stress through mindfulness like exercise, gratitude journaling, and meditation.
3. Know if your company has an anti-bullying policy and try to find out if the company actually listens to victims of workplace bullying.
4. You don't have to take it. Look for a new job if you are being bullied and can't stop it.
5. Find an outlet outside of work that makes you happy. Do as much as you can to enjoy life and don't let your job become your life.

Alan Eisenberg is a certified Life and Solutions-focused coach with a niche in bullying and abuse recovery. He is also the founder of Bullying Recovery LLC and author of "A Ladder In The Dark: My journey from bullying to self-acceptance," and "Crossing the Line." He has been writing and speaking to various audiences about the issue of C-PTSD and Bullying Recovery. Mr. Eisenberg has been featured on several prints, radio shows and podcasts on this issue, including NPR and the Boston Globe.

TWENTY-TWO

NO ACTION TAKEN – WORKPLACE BULLYING AND MOBBING IN AN ACTIVE ADULT COMMUNITY
Anonymous

I was the Fitness Director, managing the fitness activities of an over 55-active adult community with over 1,500 residents for over 4 years. A campus environment, it included condominium buildings and a clubhouse which had a restaurant, health club, aerobics studio, indoor pool, auditorium and other amenities. There was a homeowner's association governance HOA (10-resident volunteers) and a property management staff.

There was no human resources department on site and the general manager represented himself as HR. There was little or no formal employee training on employment and labor laws, OSHA, EEOC, or other policies. There were many family members employed there. The manager rarely gave positive credit to the staff and I noticed even after working on major projects, his praises were very minimal. I noticed immediately in weekly staff meetings and even during lunch breaks he routinely made disrespectful and insulting criticisms and demeaning comments. He fostered and allowed an overall unprofessional office atmosphere such as failing to address a coworker's excessive and lewd profanity and alcohol consumption in the office. I noticed and strongly sensed that another coworker was especially rude and hostile to me in weekly staff meetings. This coworker would call my fitness suggestions "dumb," "stupid" and "silly." This coworker would frequently roll her eyes and give glaring stares and scowls in meetings. She had a very negative attitude, a sense of entitlement, extreme arrogance and it was as if she wanted everything managed her way, even though she wasn't in charge. This coworker was constantly interfering in my work, trying to question, undermine, take credit and even sabotage my efforts. She lied about my work and diminished my suggestions for improvements. We were to work as a "team," but I soon realized it was all about what she wanted. I repeatedly asked her to stop interfering in my job, but she was relentless.

One early afternoon I walked by the coworker's office and saw a bottle of red wine on the desk and the coworker was drinking wine in front of another employee! I was shocked as this violated the personnel policy handbook (termination upon 1st offense) and I was also waiting on this coworker for work projects that seemed to be intentionally delayed! The next day I emailed the manager of this disturbing incident; however, he responded in writing that he had, "No issue or concerns" with an occasional cup of wine if it were after management office closing hours (4:30 pm). However, many employees, including myself, were still working and there were many residents still present in the clubhouse until 9 pm. I was shocked at his irresponsible handling of this situation. On another occasion I reported it again, and the manager asked, "Why do YOU have a problem with them drinking?" I told him that it violated personnel policies! The alcohol consumption in the office went on for years, sometimes in front of the manager and other employees, and nothing was ever done to hold anyone accountable. For me and for other coworkers, this created a very unprofessional and toxic work environment. Other employees also reported to me witnessing the wine consumption, even at various evening events that this coworker was supervising.

One day I discovered and was very upset to find graphic pornography downloaded on my work computer and though I reported it to the manager, there was no sense of urgency or formal investigation. I was frequently going to the manager with my escalating problems with this coworker. Nothing improved and instead, I was screamed at in closed-door meetings with the manager. Once I was in his office for over 1 hour with this type of abusive behavior. I felt physically sick afterwards and thought I would faint. After 4 years of feeling frustrated, disrespected and so stressed by the escalating hostility and fear, I made the decision to resign. The residents were very upset and over 200 residents petitioned for me to stay and rescind my resignation. They also asked for a meeting with the manager for the reasons of my resignation. After this meeting, the manager asked me to reconsider and stay. I told him that I wanted to inform the 10-member board of my concerns about what was going on in the office so that they could possibly help me and enforce the association policies. I filed a "Hostile/Toxic Work Environment" complaint and addressed many violations in the personnel policy manual to the board and their attorneys. The board's response was "NO ACTION TAKEN." The manager and the coworker were quite angry that I had addressed these concerns and the coworker started screaming at me that I had talked to the attorneys. The manager told me that, "All of the residents would think ill of me if I stayed." The manager, board and attorneys did not uphold the personnel policy handbook; especially, where there was a ZERO tolerance for alcohol consumption. I felt retaliated against for reporting multiple violations of policies. The health fair day was another horrific experience of mobbing, work interference and sabotage by both the manager and this coworker. I strongly suspected that another coworker was also involved. One resident begged me not to sue the association after I confided in her about the many work problems I was experiencing. Another resident advised me to "get out" before it seriously impacted my health. The last week of my employment was extremely stressful as there were more incidents of sabotage with someone changing my password on my computer so that I could not access it. My computer and desk were tampered with and items taken. I suffered great stress, many sleepless nights, anxiety, depression and resigned from my job because of the stress and fear. Many times, I cried and asked, "Why is this happening to me, WHY?"

How did I survive and cope with this for over 4 years? It was quite difficult. I prayed to God daily for protection, wisdom and peace. I tried to minimize my contact with the bully(s) in the office. With the help of a very supportive spouse, my family and friends, and advice from my physician, counselor and clergy, I slowly started to understand what was happening to me and WHY. I believe I became a target, as I was a threat to a very insecure, jealous, unprofessional, and unethical coworker who wanted to maintain her power and control. She was the weakest link in the chain called "teamwork." To help me cope, I continued my exercise as a means of managing my stress. After I resigned, I also researched workplace bullying and became very involved in anti-bullying causes that support a healthy workplace. I hope that stronger laws and policies are made to hold all companies accountable for their employee's health, well-being and SAFETY with a ZERO tolerance for bullying in the workplace. Bullying results in the loss of good employees, greater expense to companies to have to rehire and retrain staff, damages to a company's reputation, and potential expenses for litigation and liability. In my situation, my replacement was contracted and compensated $30,000 more annually, a substantial increase for the company and the residents! The new fitness director also lacked many of the qualifications of the job description and many residents complained to me (and even asked me to return!).

To this day, many of the residents have told me that they are very dissatisfied with the fitness program, unprofessional management and the weak board. Two attorneys were also hired to interview me and many other employees after I had filed a hostile/toxic work environment. Several residents have actually sold their property and moved away because they feared community liability since the ineffective board did not enforce established company policies. They worried about the potential risks for a lawsuit, safety for the other employees and the residents, with no accountability for violations, especially alcohol consumption by employees on the job. They also expressed that the community had deteriorated, no longer being as inviting and appealing to them with the lack of professional management and ethical HOA oversight. Tragically, there have been reports of employees committing suicide after experiencing bullying. All companies with the highest standards and expectations for professionalism, core values, integrity and adherence to their established policies and procedures should NEVER allow bullying practices to occur. Those who cannot uphold the company's policies and procedures should not be in positions where abuse of power, harassment and a toxic and hostile environment thrive, causing such great stress and dysfunction in the office, ultimately hurting the organization, other employees and those they work for. It is domestic abuse on the job.

My personal advice is to stand up for yourself! Bullies are diabolical thugs! Date and document every bullying event when it occurs and consult with an <u>employment attorney</u> for professional help and advice. In my situation, the Human Resources representative was totally ineffective and useless as the manager did not respect or comply with the association policies addressing the multiple reported violations, including alcohol consumption on the job. Their own personnel policy manual was a useless document and did not protect me. In retrospect, to survive workplace bullying, I would recommend:

SIX PIECES OF ADVICE:

1. Resign and find another job before the situation becomes too severe, toxic, hostile and dangerous! Remove yourself from the bully's equation. They cannot control, manipulate, sabotage, insult, demean, disrespect or abuse you any longer.
2. Take a medical leave of absence due to stress, if needed.
3. Secure the advice and counsel of an employment attorney.
4. File a complaint when you can (e.g., OSHA will investigate and address unsafe working conditions, the EEOC will help with retaliation).
5. Inform others whom you trust of what is going on so that they can help. Take good care of yourself.
6. Tell your story! You never know how your experience will help another who is going through a similar situation.

TWENTY-THREE

WHAT I LEARNED ABOUT BULLYING AND MYSELF
Peter McGarahan

My name is Pete McGarahan. I would like to share my story and what I learned about myself and how it might help others. I transferred out to a fast food restaurant (FFR) in Irvine, California in 1990 after a very successful six-year IT boot camp experience at a Fortune 500 (F500) Corporate Headquarters in Purchase, New York. I was hired as a programmer in the F500's Management Information Systems (MIS) Department after receiving my undergraduate degree in Psychology from Loyola University in Baltimore, Maryland and my Masters of Business Administration in MIS from Iona College in New Rochelle, New York. I learned everything from PL/1, COBOL and RPG-2 & RPG-3 programming languages, the IBM mainframe environment, the corporate political world and then all about the personal computer, networking and help desk/

desktop support. I quickly learned that when someone asked, "Do you know anything about...," I would quickly respond with, "I know a little about it, but I am a quick learner." I learned that there was much more to work life than technology!

At FFR, I managed the Corporate Help Desk for about a year when the new CIO asked me if I wanted to leverage my MBA and transfer to Finance and Business Planning. It was a great opportunity to learn the business, so of course I said yes. I spent two years as a Business Planner with the smartest people I had ever worked with as we grew the FFR from 1000 restaurants to over 4000 in five years. This part of my career was defined as leaving the comfort zone. It was a great learning experience but I wasn't a valued contributor. Finally, I reached out to CIO to arrange a transition back to IT. After many attempts, they finally found a position for me that leveraged none of my skills or strengths. My IT welcome home party was more like the movie Castaway starring Tom Hanks. After another round of non-value added contribution, I was transferred back to the Help Desk with the intent of being managed out of the company. My new Director had an "A-Type" personality with a reputation for being very direct and sometimes abusive. It should not have mattered because the very transparent and short-term plan was to get rid of me.

My direction was to combine the Restaurant Help Desk with the Corporate Help Desk under one best practice support model. Based on my recent experience in business and finance, I was inspired and highly motivated to approach this challenge from a perspective of business value. At the same time, I became obsessed with support industry best practices and the Help Desk Institute (HDI) was just beginning to gain traction locally and nationally. I told my new Director about my plans and he wasn't interested. I told him about a National Help Desk conference in Florida where I could get certified. I would attend best practice sessions on service and support, relevant technologies and concepts around people, development and management; again, not interested. He instructed me to send my two supervisors. Neither could attend so I decided to go myself, and not tell my director. That's when the situation got worse, much worse.

At the conference, I was amazed at how many managers were struggling to succeed. The conference was a great learning and network opportunity. I attended all the inspirational keynote, best practice, and case study sessions. I absorbed the knowledge and experience provided by the speakers. After day 2 of the conference, I went back to my hotel and there was a voice mail message from my very angry and abusive Director. He berated and cursed me out instructing me to return home immediately to face the consequences of my decision. I decided to stay for the conference party where I met wonderful people that I still am friends with today! These wonderful colleagues have positively influenced both my personal life and professional career. On the last day of the conference, they awarded the HDI Team Excellence Award. I was so impressed with the entire presentation that this experience would solidify my motivational goals and plans for the next two years.

Back at FFR headquarters, my Director not only had the pleasure (his only) of putting me in place but also telling me that I had little time left with the company. I decided that I would continue to meet with him weekly, although he did all the talking and was not interested in anything I had to say. I let him be the "Energy Vampire" that he was and suck every ounce of energy, motivation I had in me with every meeting and encounter. I spent all my time building my leadership team and assessing our current operational performance against the HDI team excellence criteria. We created a continuous service improvement road map based on what I learned at the HDI Conference that would strongly position us to compete for the HDI Team Excellence Award in 1995. In the meantime, Mr. "Let me make you feel bad so that I can feel better about myself" continued the dreaded "Nibbling," trying to damage and deplete my motivation.

Fast-forward 18 months: continuous service improvement plan was implemented and results measured and reported. The HDI Team Excellence Award nomination document was completed and sent to the HDI Team Excellence Nomination Board. A few months later, we were notified that the FFR team was selected as one of the finalist for the Team Excellence Award. My team graciously requested that I represent them for the final interview with the HDI Team Excellence Nomination Board. I actually told my Director all of this but he was no longer focused on me or my team; he had other easier targets to smack down and the 'demons' that haunted his consciousness and his ability to be human.

I flew to Florida to meet with the HDI Team Excellence Nomination Board. The room was filled with the industry luminaries who created the best practice foundation for HDI and the service and support industry. They grilled me for three hours on our nomination document confidently ensuring that everything we said we did in the document was executed the right way and yielded the expected results. The following day my team and I sat in the front row with the other finalist team members and the Executive Director of HDI took the stage. Thinking back two years ago at this time and place when I was in a positon of isolation and now I was here with my leadership team proudly and patiently waiting for the announcement of the 1995 HDI Team Excellence Award. The Executive Director opened the letter and announced that the winner was the FFR TEAM! Proudly standing at the podium with my team behind me, we accepted the trophy and the honor of the award as I reflected on the highlights of our maturity journey to the 3,000+ members in the audience.

After enjoying a few days of celebration, I returned home and went to work the next day. Our Marketing Department had created a congratulations banner for us that was proudly displayed as we walked into the building. I immediately went into my Director's office who was surprisingly happy to see me. I presented him with our 1995 HDI Team Excellence Award and told him that the award was for him but we would keep the experience and the honor of winning the award. I told him that I had learned a great deal in working for him the last two years. The biggest thing I learned was that telling me I can't do something is the best motivational force for doing it and proving him wrong.

FIVE PIECES OF ADVICE:

1. Believe in yourself – you are the driving force for making the right things happen in your life.
2. Don't let anybody say you can't do something – you can make it happen if you want to.
3. Be passionate about what you believe in and what you want to do.
4. Make your customer your support champion because you deliver.
5. Become an expert at something.

CPSIA information can be obtained
at www.ICGtesting.com
Printed in the USA
BVHW09s0838090718
521160BV00032B/1674/P